THE
HYBRID
DESIGNER

THE HYBRID DESIGNER

My Life in Sales and Design

A Memoir

Bea Gardner

Book Design & Production:
Columbus Publishing Lab
www.ColumbusPublishingLab.com
LCCN: 2025903810

Copyright © 2025 by
Bea Gardner

All rights reserved.
This book, or parts thereof, may not be
reproduced in any form without permission.

With a few exceptions where explicit permissions were
granted to use real names, the names of individuals mentioned
herein have been changed to protect personal privacy.

Paperback ISBN: 978-1-63337-922-0
Hardcover ISBN: 978-1-63337-923-7
E-Book ISBN: 978-1-63337-924-4

Printed in the United States of America
1 3 5 7 9 10 8 6 4 2

This book is dedicated to
Gordon Schiffman,
My mentor, my inspiration,
and my friend.

CONTENTS

Introduction 1
Chapter 1   Hello Gordy 4
Chapter 2   Getting to Know You 11
Chapter 3   Sales Floor Shenanigans 18
Chapter 4   Thomasville Tour 26
Chapter 5   Glen Makes Matzo Ball Soup 34
Chapter 6   Fragile Egos and Friendships 37
Chapter 7   Me and My Magazines 45
Chapter 8   Sometimes It's Just Not Easy 54
Chapter 9   Dress For Success 63
Chapter 10   The Interior Design Society 71
Chapter 11   To Sell or Dust...That Is The Question ... 82
Chapter 12   Change is in The Air...Thomas Ruff 91
Chapter 13   Pepto Bismol Pink 101
Chapter 14   UFOs and Satisfied Customers 109
Chapter 15   Back To White's and Bea Goes Greek ... 117
Chapter 16   Thurber House 126
Chapter 17   My Park Towers Adventure 134
Chapter 18   The End of an Era 145
Afterword 155
Acknowledgements 163
About the Author 165

INTRODUCTION

The Hybrid Designer talks about me and my "wanna-be" designer dream. I came from a modest background, with no degree, and became one of the most well-known Interior Designers in Columbus, Ohio, in a field that mostly catered to the affluent.

When I lost my father at the age of 14, my childhood came to an end. My older brother and I were thrown into the workforce to be able to buy things like school clothes and have spending money. My dad was 35 years old and had no life insurance when he died unexpectedly, leaving my mom a widow with five children under the ages of 15. My oldest brother and I contributed part of our incomes to help our mother financially.

I married at the age of 19 while most of my high school friends were finishing their first year of college. Three years into the marriage, I gave birth to my first child, William who was

INTRODUCTION

named after my father. That was when my husband insisted that I no longer work. That's just the way it was back then. "A woman's place was in the home."

I immersed myself into the world of Art and Design and home furnishings while fulfilling my new role of motherhood and homemaker. Our second son, Glen, was born three and a half years later. During those early years of motherhood, I took art classes in painting, sculpture, pottery and art history from some of the best art teachers in the area. While my kids were in school, I browsed through furniture stores, shopping for furnishings for our new home, and I especially loved a place called Garth Andrews Interiors and Design. Because of my accumulated art and furniture background, I began to dream of becoming a decorator. But, my husband did not allow me to work. It was out of the question, however I did enter a decorating contest and the winner got to keep all the furniture and accessories in the room that was submitted in the contest. I won this contest.

A few years later, I found myself in the throes of a divorce. I had no real work experience after having my children. That was when I got an ultimatum from my divorce lawyer. "Without a job, the judge will not grant you your divorce," he said. He told me I would need proof that I will be able to support myself and my children. It was that circumstance that forced me to seek employment.

Under pressure, and at a time when I was not at my best, I had the presence of mind to reach deep within to find a way to try to become what I always wanted to become, an Interior Designer. I contacted the furniture buyers of the department store where I won the decorating contest, and they came to my rescue. They pulled strings and helped me land my first job in the business, and the rest is history.

As you turn the pages, you will learn how two design competitions and one lucky lottery brought me full circle in the world of design in Columbus.

Little did I know what struggles lie ahead. Being a woman with aspirations in a career, and being a single parent, was almost an insurmountable task during those years.

The Hybrid Designer is a memoir, specifically about my long and winding road with White's Fine Furniture and other established furniture retailers, and my business relationship with Gordon Schiffman, owner of the White's dynasty with whom I credit much of my success. My memoir dabbles a bit with the struggles of raising my sons, and gives the reader a glimpse of juggling an adult "single" woman's life in spite of career and parenting and into my marriage to Steve. Thank you for reading. I look forward to sharing my story with you.

CHAPTER 1

HELLO GORDY!

While reading the Sunday paper one fine morning I saw a full page spread that got my attention. The Polsky Department Store was advertising a decorating contest to furnish a room, any room in your home. The winner of the contest would be awarded all the merchandise in the entire room. Yes, all the furniture and accessories will be given to the winner.

I was living in a large contemporary home with four bedrooms. The fourth bedroom could have been a nursery or an office or a guest room. It was an empty room. I never quite knew what I wanted the room to be. Why not, I thought. I read the ad again and decided to jump in and enter the contest. The only criterion was that every item placed in your entry had to be merchandise from the store – furniture, carpet, and accessories.

I picked up an application and entered the contest. During the next two weeks, I visited the department store almost every weekday morning while my youngest was in kindergarten, especially the furniture department. I finally came up with a plan for decorating the room. I had to enter SKU numbers for each item I selected for the room. I remember dragging my sister with me one day during this process and she thought I was crazy doing this. She thought I was wasting my time, but I pressed on. I was energized and excited. I immersed myself in this project.

I finally submitted my room plan and all the SKU numbers pertaining to my selections and left the rest for the judges. I decided to turn the room into a little upstairs den/office/guest room. I selected a sofa bed and small desk made of rosewood with chrome legs as the main furniture in my little room. Some cool accessories and lamps were the finishing touches. If I did not win the contest, we probably would have purchased most of the things I selected to complete that empty room in our house.

Several weeks later I got a call from the furniture buyers of the store with the news that I had won the contest. I was stunned to hear about my win. I had to pinch myself to see if I was awake. At the time of this call, we made arrangements to meet in person to go over the specifics. We chatted for an hour or so and ended the conversation with a delivery date. We got along famously, and it was obvious these two furniture buyers from Polsky's liked me and I liked them. I was overwhelmed with pride and excitement for this accomplishment. It was at that moment that I knew I wanted to be a real Interior Designer.

Several years had passed since that design contest. I had just divorced and needed a job. I contacted the furniture buyers and, sure enough, they remembered me. I asked if the door was still open to work for them in the furniture department. I did not know it, but they were easing out of the furniture business at Polsky's, and they could not offer me a job due to these circumstances. That was the bad news. The good news was they put me in touch with their buyer friends at the Lazarus Department Store at the Summit Mall in Akron, Ohio, just a few miles from my home. With their recommendation, I interviewed with Lazarus and was hired on the spot.

Yippee! My career was on its way. I landed the job in the sales/design department at the Lazarus Co. At the very beginning I was given a little office to do design work and design presentations if the occasion arose, but mostly my job was to be present on the sales floor. I was in seventh heaven. I was on my way.

I do recall one of my first sales at Lazarus. It's a funny story. It was a Friday evening, and a young couple bought a white bar server on wheels from me right off the floor. It was an easy sale and I was proud. After they left the store with their purchase, one of the guys who had floor duty with me that Friday evening laughed and said, "Don't count your commission on that sale." He went on to tell me that little portable bar gets sold quite often on a Friday night and gets used over the weekend and comes back on Monday as a return. Yep, he was right.

I thought things were going good after my divorce. How wrong I was. My ex found so many ways to hassle and abuse me that he made it impossible for me to live in the same town. I decided to move to Columbus, Ohio. I had a few water ski friends living there and it was far enough away from Akron that it became my destination.

While at Lazarus, I talked to my furniture rep friend, Sam, who had accounts in Akron and Columbus. I told him on the QT I was planning to make a move to Columbus and I would be looking for a job there. I was very specific about wanting to work in a store that specialized in Contemporary furnishings. I considered myself the most knowledgeable in this category of furnishings based on my many visits to Garth Andrews in Bath, Ohio.

Sam produced the name of a store called Darrens. He said he would put in a good word for me, and he said it was a slam dunk that I would get hired there. Darren's Furniture specialized in Contemporary furniture. I proceeded with my plan.

I bought a little condo in a Columbus suburb and was excited and nervous to begin this new chapter in my life. I spent the first few weeks hanging around the pool at the condo with my sons. I registered them for school and helped them get acclimated to the move. It was during that time that I chose not to jump into a new job. I was going to spend what was left of the summer with the boys in a leisurely way before I called Darrens for an interview.

During one of these sizzling summer days, I met a neighbor guy named Frank and he said everyone calls me Frankie. He too was lavishing in luxury at the pool with his two young sons while his wife was at work. We struck up a conversation and he asked what I did that would allow me the time to hang around the pool all day getting a beautiful tan. I told him I was a beach bum between jobs, and I was enjoying a few weeks doing nothing. He then asked me what kind of work I was in. I told him I was in sales and design in the furniture business. I went on to explain that I was going to look for a job when the kids went back to school.

Frankie was amazed. He told me he was in the same business. He rattled on for quite some time telling me that I should go to his store, and he would personally grease the way for a personal interview with the owner. Knowing where I had worked before moving to Columbus and what I was into, he all but guaranteed I would get hired. There was no end to his enthusiasm.

I told him thank you but no thank you because I was only interested in Contemporary furniture and that one of my rep friends had already paved the way for me to get hired at a place called Darrens. Frankie went on to tell me that White's Fine Furniture was just starting the process of separating floor space in their stores to have one section be only Contemporary furnishings and accessories.

So, after a couple of weeks of settling into my new surroundings and a few more chats with Frankie at the pool on his days off, he finally talked me into meeting his boss and giving White's a look. This was before the internet of course. You just did not go online and check them out. I did not know what to expect when I went in for my interview or how his boss would react to me, but I really did not care. Frankie told me he might only give me about five minutes of his valuable time, but do not be put off by that. That is just the way he is.

A few days later I got out of my bathing suit and donned my business/ interior design look and drove to the store to meet Frankie's boss for this apparent five-minute interview.

Mr. Schiffman was a bit intimidating when I walked into his office. He closed the door and suddenly we were talking about everything...furniture and Contemporary brands that were known to me and some of the newer brands that I was not familiar with. We talked about family, philosophy, and the art of selling furniture. We talked about some of our likes, dislikes, and hobbies, we talked on and on. We just really clicked.

After about one hour he finally said, "I really have enjoyed meeting you and I must get back to work. When can you start?" It was that simple. I had a job.

That began a long relationship with White's Fine Furniture and Gordon Schiffman. I got up to leave

Gordy

and thanked Mr. Shiffman and he said, "Please, just call me Gordy."

When I got home, I talked to the boys about my new job. Since it was the same job description that I was doing while working at Lazarus in Akron there was not much to explain. However, we talked about the adventure of meeting new people and driving a bit further to work and how we would handle my evening store hours in our household. I equated my excitement about all of this with the excitement and challenge they would soon be facing with a new school and new friends. We were all preparing to dig our heels into our new surroundings.

By this time I had met my neighbors and I found a very nice high school girl to watch over the boys during my absent hours at home. Bill was 12 years old at that time and Glen three and a half years younger.

CHAPTER 2

GETTING TO KNOW GORDY

Two weeks after Gordy hired me, the boys started back to school and I started my new job. It was the start of my long off and on relationship with White's and Gordy. I spent most of my first two weeks on the job in the upstairs balcony of the newly designed Contemporary section of the Morse Road store. Gordy and I tagged and priced the furniture and accessories that were earmarked for the new Contemporary section of White's. I cleaned sticky labels off glass top tables, hung tags, and wrote out the tickets.

Gordy gave me the code word for pricing. What does that mean to you? Well, the word for pricing went like this. The code was "washingtol." Each letter of the word stood for a number. If a table cost the company $25.00 the code would be AILL. A stood for the number 2 and the letter I stood for the number 5 and the letter L stood for the number 0. Thus, that table cost the company $25.00. The code was put on the back of each sales slip and the retail price is what the public saw. It was tricky for me to get this in my mind quickly, so I devised a cheat sheet with the word "washingtol" with the corresponding number written above each letter. Whew, I was catching on.

Seems like pricing and making tickets for each piece of furniture to be placed in the proper settings in the store might have been boring to some people. I found this task very exciting. I not only got to see and touch the new merchandise that I would be selling, but I also had the opportunity to become an expert on most everything contemporary in the company and played a part in setting up the room settings.

It was also interesting and exciting to work so closely with Gordy. He was dynamic and oozed with charm, and handsome too I might add. I sometimes found myself "crushing" on him. I made up my mind early on to suppress that feeling. I can assure you nothing was ever going to happen in any way other than a business relationship. I knew from the start he was a happily married man and he always addressed his wife as "Lovey" when they talked on the phone.

I remember Gordy asking me how I came to know the brand names of Contemporary furniture. I told him about Garth Andrew Interiors. They were located very close to where I lived in Akron and I told him while my friends were shopping for the latest style in clothing I was shopping for furniture at Garth Andrew. It was like being in a museum. It was there that I educated myself to Contemporary design and quality furniture. I told him how I poured over catalogs and finally bought my first piece of solid wood furniture. I bought a Founders dining room table and chairs and a matching buffet and server.

Garth Andrews...my favorite hangout

I could tell Gordy was impressed because he was nodding his head as I spoke. During these kinds of conversations, I threw in a couple of other name brands like a Knoll table that I bought. Yes, Gordy was impressed. At the same time, he introduced me to DIA, Design Institute of America, a metal and glass table line of furniture. Later in my employ, I bought a DIA chrome and glass cocktail table. Loved it. I was also introduced to the "playpen" sofa. A large modular upholstered piece of furniture. I quickly learned to show how they would lay out on the in store graph paper tablets. I believe I sold more playpens than any other salesperson in the entire company.

The boys and I spent a weekend in Akron for a visit before the new job and the start of school. On the return trip two blocks from home at 1:30 in morning, the kids asleep in the back seat of the car, I got stopped for speeding. Cop was nice, he felt sorry for me with two kids asleep in the car and my story and he let me go. Whew. I dodged a ticket.

Gordy and I worked for two weeks on the balcony tagging and marking the furniture according to shipping papers, when out of the blue Gordy said, "Bea, how would you like an opportunity to make a little money this weekend? We're having a warehouse sale and I would like to put you on the sales floor. Everything you sell will be added towards your commission." I said, "Sounds good to me." He gave me the time and the address on West Broad Street and I was to show up on Sunday at noon.

Well, being new in town and having never driven to the downtown area I made sure I got directions. Remember, this was before cell phones and GPS. I followed the directions given to me by my new friend Frankie from my condo and I set off to get to the warehouse store a little early so as not to get lost.

I drove downtown with directions from Frankie and made my right turn off High Street to Broad with hardly a car in sight. I no sooner turned and what did I see. OMG. Flashing lights. I got pulled over. Apparently, the sign on the light said no right turn. Yep, you guessed it. I was handed a traffic violation for making a right turn on Broad Street from High Street.

The cop was mean. I guess he had nothing better to do on a quiet Sunday morning. I tried to explain to him that I was new in town, had never driven to this area before and that I was on my way to White's Furniture as a salesperson for their big Sunday sale. I told him there was no one in sight and I never thought for one moment that I was breaking the law. I pleaded with him to not give me a ticket to no avail. So that is the way I went to the warehouse sale to make extra money and now whatever I might make will be needed to pay the traffic ticket. A bad start on the sales floor, that is for sure. I did not dodge that bullet like I did only two weeks previously.

Since this was my first sales opportunity in my new job I tried to put the ticket incident aside and get out there and sell, sell, sell. Selling at the warehouse was a little hard at first but I recall selling a bedroom set and it probably took me a little longer than most to write up the order. I was getting into sales mode. At that stage in my career, I was relegated to selling, not designing.

A little while later in the day I had a customer, and I had to excuse myself for a moment to ask the manager of the store a question pertaining to this potential sale. I told the customer I would be right back with an answer. When I got back to that customer just minutes later, I saw this big fat salesman with a beard moving in on my customer. When I approached them, he looked at me and in a very sweet voice he said, "Don't worry about this, I got you covered." And just like that he stole a sale from me. That was my introduction to Kenny.

Well, between making furniture tags with Gordon and helping to set up the new merchandise during my first two weeks, getting a traffic ticket and having a sale stolen from me by Kenny, I began to realize I was moving in the wrong direction towards making money. I had to figure out a way to deal with life at White's. I came down off the balcony most afternoons late in the day to hit the sales floor. During this time, I began to acquaint myself with my fellow sales associates. I never had any regrets about not interviewing at Darrens because I soon came to think of White's as my home away from home.

I thought about those first few weeks and concluded that helping Gordy prepare the Contemporary section for the opening of the Contemporary Store was my priority and my pleasure. I figured that instead of being thrown right onto the sales floor and swimming with the sharks I would continue this snail's pace to make money and just keep on chugging along.

This whole beginning has always been to my advantage over the years. I not only became an expert in that section of the store, but I also had the opportunity to bond with the boss in a very personal way. If I had been hired and thrown onto the sales floor without getting to know Gordy, I probably would not have loved my job and respected him as much as I did.

It was during this time that in a casual conversation with Gordy as we were tagging merchandise that I mentioned son number one was nearing his Bar Mitzvah. I told Gordy they asked me for the names of the two people who I had selected to sit on the Bema with him and I told the Rabbi I did not have anyone who comes to mind other than my brother and that I did not want my ex husband to be up there.

The next day while on the balcony working with Gordy, he asked me if I had figured out yet who would be sitting up on the stage with Bill during his Bar Mitzvah. "No," I said, "probably no one other than my brother." It was then that Gordy offered to be that person. He said he belonged to the Temple and it would be his pleasure. It was a very heart-warming moment and I was proud as punch to have his presence up there. My family seemed pleased too. They seemed to think my move to Columbus might work out.

There was a very distinguished gentleman who came up to me after the ceremony and congratulated me for the performance by the Bar Mitzvah boy. I thanked him and said, "I'm sorry, I don't think I know you. Have we ever met?" He told me he was the recently retired Rabbi from this Temple. I was so embarrassed that I did not know who he was. "Don't worry, Mom," he said, "your son did a great job and by the way, how do you know Gordon?" I told him I work for White's and he said how pleased he was to meet me.

As you read further you will realize there were times when I did not like some things about Gordy and even when those times occurred, I always loved him. He was kind and genuine and personable to me, and always seemed to have an interest in my life and my family. Yes, Gordy was special.

CHAPTER 3

SALES FLOOR SHENANIGANS

I had the late shift tonight. It was a slow Thursday evening. Our manager, Larry, took his dinner hour and as he was walking out the door, he chastised us for hanging around the front door looking like a bunch of car salesmen. He then gave us our marching orders. A new Pennsylvania House bedroom set had just been placed on the floor and he told us to accessorize it in our spare time that evening.

That meant we had to adorn the room with a bedspread, pillows, lamps, pictures, etc. I loved doing that because it was a design-oriented task. Lou, one of my fellow sales associates, went to work pricing and tagging the set and a couple of us set about with the accessorizing. We picked out a bedspread from the back room, set out the lamps on the two nightstands, and got to work with the finishing touches. Pretty soon it was my "up" and I left that task.

After my "up" left the store, I had to pick a few tchotchkes* to finish the room display. Now, picture this. I found a plaster bust of Adonis on the shelf in one of the wall units in another section of the store. I carefully placed that head on the pillow of the bedroom set, face up, and pulled the bedspread around it to make it look like a head was asleep on the pillow. I then found one other accessory to add to the vignette. It was a bud vase that I positioned under the bed spread about halfway down from the head of Adonis. The visual of that bed spoke loud and clear. Adonis was having a wet dream. I said to myself, *oh no Bea, you can't do this. You have gone too far!*

I asked my fellow floor friends to come over and check out the accessory job I did. I told them it was a bit unusual, and I wanted their opinion. They saw it and roared with laughter. I said I would take out the vase and leave Adonis to sleep on the bed that night. After our good laugh they all decided that I should leave the vase in for Larry's reaction when he came back into the store. I agreed to leave it that way if all of us would take credit for the accessory job. I did not want that to fall on my shoulders alone. Everyone agreed and we left things as is. Gordy never entered the store through the Pennsylvania House doors, so I was certain he would never see the accessory job we did on that bedroom set. Just saying.

Not all things that went on during floor hours were funny and fun like the one I just described. At one time or another we all had reasons to complain about retail hours. Kenny complained about having to work when his son was playing little league ball that evening, but the minute he had a good up the complaining would stop. That was Kenny, always hungry for an opportunity to make a sale. Lots of us moaned about working on a holiday Sunday like the 4th of July. We could not have picnics with family and friends. We never could celebrate New Years days because Gordy always spent big bucks advertising huge sales on holiday weekends.

Whatever the situation, working until nine o'clock in the evening, most weekends and holidays, selling furniture when most of the world is at home doing things with family and friends is just the way it is in this business. Couples that shop for furniture generally only shop after they have had dinner and they have put their busy work days behind them. And holidays give them the time to visit a furniture store. Working evenings and holiday hours in this business is a key to success.

I loved meeting and greeting a couple who were genuinely interested in why they were in a furniture store, and I especially enjoyed the challenge of figuring out who the decision maker was in the pair. Sometimes I even asked the question like this: "Hey, which one of you is really the one making the decision on the color of this sofa?" Most of the time the guy would say, "That's her department, I just pay for it" and that brings me to the part of the sale where I try to figure out who holds the purse strings. That is when I can begin to close in on the sale. Sometimes that answer flows during the process with a comment from the hubby where he says something like, "Whatever she wants, I only pay for it." That immediately lets me know who the decision maker is and who pays for the furniture.

It's not always that cut and dried. I remember one of my early design jobs that I almost didn't get because I didn't figure out this part of the sale early on. This couple came to my store with the anticipation of not liking what I had put together for them and they started to argue. He didn't like this and she didn't like that and they bickered about everything. The house had floor to ceiling rough-sawn cedar wood in a herringbone pattern on the fireplace and the beautiful golf course with all its greenery was visible through the windows. I chose a very natural pallet with a bit of a rustic look and the lady of the house wanted the whole house done in pastels…what we called the "ice cream colors" in the business.

They continued to argue and fight in my office and I finally said, "Hey, let's just call this quits. I don't think I can satisfy you guys and no hard feelings, but you are free to leave." As the doctor got up to go, she grabbed him by the collar and dragged him back into my office.

Everyone calmed down and we decided to give it another chance and do the house in the pastel colors to her liking. *Ugh*, I thought, but I worked closely with the Mrs. during the next month and if I may say so myself, I pulled it off. As I recall, we took out the floor to ceiling herringbone rough sawn cedar fireplace in the dining room and mirrored the entire fireplace, floor to ceiling, in the same herringbone design that was in the cedar wood. The living room side of the fireplace was just drywall painted in one of the pastel colors with a beautiful picture hanging over it. This color scheme started to come together.

I learned while working with her that they were Greek, and she wanted a more ethnic colorful look in their home. When I gave the final presentation to both about a month later, I was surprised to learn that the Mr. was very satisfied and took to her colorful scheme with no arguments. Looking at the finished product with the mauve colored leather on the six fully upholstered dining chairs in the mirrored floor to ceiling fireplace was a striking sight to behold in the dining room.

What I also learned from that initial fight in my office was who held the purse strings. Even though he was a doctor it was the lady of the house who had the money. We became very close during the month that she and I were putting the look together when she told me money was no object because she was spending a portion of her inheritance on the re-do of the house. We all became friends, and I was even invited to their daughter's wedding at the country club where they lived. It turned out to be a happily ever after story that started from a bad beginning. I use this as an example of why you should not prejudge who holds the purse strings in a sale.

I had another design job where both the husband and wife probably could afford what they came to have me accomplish, which was to fully furnish their living room. They were both lawyers. She was teaching law at a university and he was just starting out in his practice and they had a beautiful home in Arlington, a suburb of Columbus. I went out to measure the room and look at surrounding furnishings to get a feel for direction.

There was a sunroom which was next to the living room in full view. It was furnished in college type furnishings and had a very cluttered, tacky look which would make anything I did in the living room NOT look good so I quickly measured the room and said I would do the best I could. I mentioned to them that I felt it necessary to incorporate the sunroom in my presentation because they almost needed to be treated as one room. We scheduled the presentation two weeks out and I left knowing I had my work cut out for myself

I put the two rooms together as one visual which really stepped up the whole downstairs with a very complete look. The presentation went very well, and they truly liked everything I did, however they hesitated to do the rooms. Apparently, the Mr. had wanted to purchase a BMW car, and she wanted to spend the money on the newly designed rooms. They were struggling with the decision, and I stepped in and put it this way. I said, "If you purchase the furnishings necessary to complete the two rooms it will be a lifetime purchase. You will be proud to entertain your friends and family in the beautiful surroundings. If you choose to buy a brand-new car instead you will enjoy the smell of the new car for a while, and it will seem new for about a year then it will soon no longer be a new car. A few years down the road it will soon be an old car and need to be replaced. I can assure you that this furniture will last as long as you want it to last and you can both take pride in what you have done to beautify your home for many years." I then told them to make the decision and get back to me.

At the onset of greeting this couple I did not know I was competing with his desire to get that BMW first as he began to rise in his career or if furnishing their living room would win out. I was very fond of these two young attorneys when I met them and especially when I visited their beautiful home while I was there measuring.

They went home, pondered, and called me the next day and said they will spend the money on doing the living room and sunroom and will not be purchasing the new BMW. I was so happy for them and happy for my commission check to come in when everything was delivered from this job.

Later, when I needed an attorney, Tommy was the one. We remained friends long after the sale.

It was about this time in my employment that my ex stopped paying me child support for about eight months and I was a bit strapped for cash so I worked on Rosh Hashanah, one of the holiest of holy days in the Jewish calendar. One of my co-workers questioned me as to why I was working on this day. I told her G-d would forgive me for working on this day because he knew I did not want to lose the opportunity of adding to my income to support my family. Furthermore, I told Mary, this holiday was a day of atonement and I told her that I did not sin this year so I had nothing to atone for. I said to her, I did not break any of the ten commandments so I am working. She was very religious and did not buy into my reasoning. She asked me if I had ever lusted for a man during this past year and she stopped me in my tracks. I nodded and said, "You win. I guess I have sinned" and with that I left the conversation because I was called to greet the next customer that would walk through our doors.

*tchotchke - A tchotchke (/ˈtʃɒtʃkə/ CHOTCH-kə, /ˈtʃɒtʃkiː/ CHOTCH-kee) is a small bric-à-brac or miscellaneous item.

CHAPTER 4

THOMASVILLE TOUR

I thought, *OMG Bea, you're always junking and thrifting*, as I bent over to pick up a scrap of wood that was lying on the floor in the wood carving building on our Thomasville tour.

We were grouped around a huge, computerized lathe and watched with interest the carving of a chair part. I remember the tour guide telling us how they dried out the hardwood before it was doweled, glued and screwed into a sofa frame. The Thomasville tour guide stopped our group to watch the lathe carve out a chair part. That was when I noticed a carving of a chair back lying on the floor. It was beautiful but I am sure it was flawed in some way and that is why it was considered scrap. I picked it up off the floor and had intended to keep it as a souvenir. I really liked it. The tour guide saw me pick it up and he said we are not allowed to pick up and keep any scraps like that… so I put it back. *Hmmm*, I thought. I really wanted that piece of carved wood, so I lingered in the back of the group as we moved on and when I knew no one was watching I went back and picked it up.

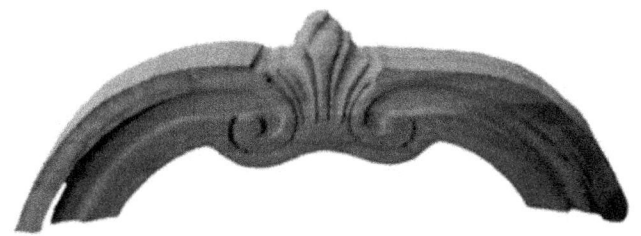

The woodcarving piece that I picked up off the floor at the Thomasville factory.

I also picked up a chair leg off the floor too. I quickly put them in my Thomasville tote bag that I carried around while touring. To this very day I still have the two flawed, raw wood items that I picked up off the floor while touring Thomasville. With fond memories, I love looking at them on my bookshelf as a decorative item.

In January of 1981, 22 of us boarded the Armstrong private jet for Thomasville, North Carolina to tour the Thomasville manufacturing facility. I don't know how Gordy chose who would go and who would be left behind to mind the stores but there we were, all lined up for our tour picture in Thomasville, NC. I remember my dear friend Jean was not on that plane with the rest of us. I felt sad because she was not making the trip. I do recall my excitement about being chosen to go and I later learned from Jean that she was terrified of flying. That's

Thomasville Tour

why she passed on this opportunity to watch furniture being manufactured. She never told anyone but me why she did not attend and I kept her secret (until now!).

Shortly after our return, while Jean and I spent our lunch hour at Stan's, I remember telling her the story of my picking up the scrap of carving while eating our fish sandwich and making sure to save room for Stan's lemon meringue pie. Jean was very straight-laced and, as I recall, she laughed out loud when I told her the story of my stowing that scrap of wood in my tote bag.

At another lunch at Tee Jays…formerly Jerry's restaurant located on Morse Road and High Street, I went on to babble about the airplane ride to Thomasville during that dinner hour at Jerry's. I guess I was trying to tell my friend that it was not much different than driving in her camper.

The airplane was quite different from any commercial aircraft, I told her. The interior layout was the most obvious difference. The seating was set up in a conversational manner and as I recall, the seats were positioned in groups of four with a table in the middle, much like sitting around the kitchen table in swivel chairs. Soon after takeoff we were each given a Thomasville tote bag filled with goodies. Enclosed in our goodie bag was a deck of cards with the Armstrong Logo. I believe that was the first time I became aware the Armstrong Flooring Company owned Thomasville Furniture Industries.

We all settled in for a smooth flight and some of us, me included, played a little Euchre on the plane with one of the deck of cards that someone opened. I kept mine in the wrappings and I never unwrapped my souvenir Armstrong deck.

Columbus was having extremely cold weather that January. The temperature the week before our scheduled trip dipped down to -4 below zero. It presented a bit of a problem for me to decide what to pack for this trip knowing that the temperature in Raleigh was in the 50's. It was almost convertible weather in Raleigh, I thought as I was packing.

Our White's group of 22 were met at the airport by a tour bus and drove us the 32 miles to Thomasville, North Carolina. Our tour began with a wonderful lunch and the two-day red-carpet tour of the Thomasville factories. I say factories because Thomasville consisted of several different buildings taking us through the many stages of furniture making.

Of course, I was fascinated by the design department. We viewed a room full of designers with their heads bent over their drawing boards. I can only imagine how difficult it must be to take a design from a collection and marry it into the entire collection, i.e. bedroom sets including headboards, tables, dining rooms and dining room chairs. The entire collection, whether white'sit be French Provincial or Contemporary, had to be designed as a collection, not just one piece of furniture.

The upholstery department was a symphony of fabrics and talented craftsmen putting the fabrics on the wood frames. We watched the precision that was taken to match stripes and plaids from the back of the sofa to the cushion and the skirt. The entire process was a work of art.

Thomasville Tour

The last building we toured was to complete the last stage of the wood collections, the finish stage. We were told that from start to finish the surface of a dining room table went through 22 layers of finish, everything from sanding the piece of product to the many layers of paints and stains down to the hand rubbed coats of lacquers and varnishes.

All in all, the red-carpet tour gave us a lot of confidence that we were selling a high-end piece of furniture. And White's was exclusive in the Columbus area with the Thomasville line.

Professional Retail Sales Seminar
White's
January 14–15, 1981

That's me in the center front row. I was 41 years old with a patch of white hair at the time of this trip to Thomasville. I wore a pair of Khaki slacks with a blazer and silk blouse with a bow under a vest. I topped off this layered look with a string of pearls overlapping the bow in my blouse. I had been at White's about 6 years when we were pictured for this trip. I guess I was considered an old timer by then.

A lot of the Blue Blazer Brigade showed up in the men's attire. That never surprised me.

Andy, Gordy's youngest son, was fresh out of college and was dressed in his usual preppy look. I noticed him taking a lot of notes. I'm sure he was going to relay every move we made to Daddy. I can just imagine the smile Gordy would have had if Andy were to tattle about me getting chastised for picking up that scrap of wood.

I did a little daydreaming on the return flight about driving my "cool" Dodge convertible while thinking of warmer weather. I love cars and have had many, however the car that I owned that year was my favorite. It was a white Dodge LaBaron convertible with saddle colored leather interior. I bought it in the spring, and I remember Gordy commenting on my car. He seemed to be infatuated with it so one day I said to him, "Why don't you take it for a spin? I think you might be surprised how comfortable it is." He said I might take you up on that someday. By the way, I had vanity plates on my car. The plates read BEA 8. People would ask me what the 8 stood for. I just told them it was because my car ran on BEA 8 juice.

Gordy also had vanity plates on his little Mercedes convertible. It was silver in color with navy blue leather seats. I guess it suited him. However, watching a tall guy like him

Thomasville Tour

getting in and out of that little toy looked to be a bit awkward. But, then again, it was a Mercedes and Gordy sure did like the sporty look. It was always parked in the spot by the front entrance to the store.

When I arrived at work the day after our trip to Thomasville, I pulled up to a beautiful car exactly like mine that was painted black with saddle colored leather interior. Wow, I thought, I wish I could have afforded the "Woody" model like this one. I got out of my car and decided to walk around that beautiful black "Woody" and almost fainted when I saw Gordy's vanity plates on the car. OMG, he did it. He bought the same exact car as mine only with the upgrade in price to the "Woody" model. I couldn't believe it, I thought, as I walked right to his office and stuck my head in the doorway and said to Gordy, "Nice car."

So, while I was touring Thomasville, Gordy was touring the Dodge dealership.

I was glad to be back in my routine and things were going along well. Or so I thought. Just when you least expect it a problem comes your way. I got a phone call one evening at work. The call was from one of Billy's classmates' mother. She said, "Are you Bill Gardner's mother?" "Yes," I said. "Well," she said in a rather condescending voice, "did you know your son is growing marijuana in the basement of your house?" Needless to say, that was one of many things I had to confront Bill with over the years. When I think back on it I had to laugh. He was always entrepreneurial. I took the bull by the horns when I got home that night. I told him about the phone call and we went down to the section of the basement with the dirt floor. I stood down there with my arms folded watching him dismantle his marijuana farm that he had assembled in the basement of our 100 year old home that I was remodeling. Glen was very quiet through the whole process. That's all I'm going to say about this. No wonder my hair was graying.

CHAPTER 5

GLEN MAKES MATZO BALL SOUP

Not every client is easy. I was trying to satisfy a very well-known guy who owned a chain of restaurants around town and he recently got divorced. He always came in about 8:45 in the evening when we closed at 9. I remember him asking me to have a drink with him after closing and I quickly put that to rest. "No thank you," I said. I always go straight home after my late shift to be with my sons before bedtime. I also told him I did not appreciate these late-night appointments. He took offense to both and I never did get the job of decorating or selling him furniture. I said a happy farewell to that potential client.

Working retail hours often wreaked havoc on my personal life. I talked to the boys almost every evening at around 6:00. We chatted about their day. How did you do in your wrestling match, how was your day at school, are you going to Harold's house, be home before dark, etc. Quite often, Billy would ask me how to cook something. If I bought ground beef, he would ask me how to make a meatloaf or spaghetti. I always gave him directions and he became a fabulous cook.

Quite often, my manager would walk past me, shake his finger and mouth the word "no." He would later tell me we are not supposed to be spending time on personal phone calls.

After a few of his scoldings for my doing this, I went to Gordy and told him my story. I told Gordy that when I'm at work during my two evenings a week I spend a little time with my sons on the phone when I do not have a customer. He said, "Don't worry Bea, I'll tell Larry that you are free to talk to your kids anytime." *Thank you Gordy*, I said to myself.

There was one time when I was getting more than the usual amount of calls from the boys. They had decided to prepare the Seder meal for Passover. I was working but I guided them through the entire process. Billy did most of the cooking but Glen was so proud to have made the Matzo Ball Soup. He followed the directions on the box. I made sure all the ingredients needed for the meal were bought before I went off to work.

Now here's the interesting part of the Seder. There was only one other Jewish family at their school so Bill invited them to attend our Seder. Glen loved his teacher who was an Italian Jew from New York and she too was invited.

I came home from work to find the table set to perfection with the Seder prayer books, the Haggadah, at every place setting. I had a real Passover Seder put together from start to finish by the boys while I was at work at White's. Yes, there were many phone calls to me to make this happen but it was a Passover to remember.

To this very day, Glen is still in touch with his teacher friend and we all stay in touch with the family they invited to share our Passover feast. I was never so proud of my boys.

CHAPTER 6

FRAGILE EGOS & FRIENDSHIPS

Soon after I started working for White's, Gordy introduced me to Joyce. He introduced her as one of his designers. I later found out that she did not sell from the floor. She called herself a designer and floor sales did not suit her, however the money she earned from White's came from merchandise she sold to complete her design jobs. Gordy accepted her on her terms because he only had to pay her in commission for whatever she put on the books. You might say she was a freelance designer on the White's payroll. She had an office in the rear of the East store about the size of a closet, but she often visited the Morse Road store for accessories or anything else that might not be available in the East store.

Joyce decided she was going to be the one to show me around when she was in the Morse Road store and I did not fight her on that. I sometimes envied her because she was not on the sales floor with the rest of us.

Joyce and I were strolling through the store one early evening and her friend Ron was lounging on a sofa in the sleep shop. He noticed Joyce and hollered over to her, "Hello there beautiful." Joyce was happy to be the one to introduce me to her friend Ron.

She introduced me to Ron by saying, "Darling, this is Gordy's latest hire. Her name is Bea." He put his hand on his hip and slowly said, "Is your name Beatrice?" I said, "Yes, but everyone calls me Bea." He smiled and looked me right in the eye and said, "Well, from now on I will call you Bea-a trice." He went on to say, "I'm Ron, I'm a queen and I don't hide it." Ron became the only friend I ever had who called me by my given name. We became very good friends.

I remember the time Ron told me my sons were NOT gay. He picked me up to attend a White's Christmas party. We were going to go as "dates" so we could dance the night away. He came in to meet Billy and Glen. When we were in the car on our way to the party after meeting the boys, Ron said, "Beatrice, I can tell you one thing, you will not have to worry about." "What is that?" I said. "Those boys are definitely not gay," he said. I really loved Ron. He was to me the close "girlfriend" I didn't have.

It took a while, but I did form another lasting friendship with a person from White's named Jean. We had the same position at White's, that of sales and design. I loved the possibility of turning a sales customer into a design client, while Jean did the same, but she never did much in the house call area. She did most of her room layouts on the big graph tablets supplied by White's while I grew as an interior designer doing my layouts on vellum paper to a ¼ inch scale. Month after month Jean was either at the top in sales for the entire company or second only to Kenny.

Ron and Joyce both could not understand why I liked Jean. They made fun of her style of dress. I knew Joyce did it out of jealousy, but Ron was a bit surprising to me when he made fun of her, what he called, "contrived beige." Joyce could not hold a candle to Jean when it came to style. I guess that was when I learned that all of us that make up the sales floor, and especially us designers, suffer from fragile egos.

I learned from Jean that too much color in my wardrobe was not a wise way to dress as a designer. She always wore beige and I always wore jeans and I told her that I never considered denim as a color. She felt that if you wore too much color and prints when you were giving a presentation your colors would fight the colors in the fabrics you were showing. The adage, less is more, certainly fell into that category.

She taught me to love shopping at Schottenstein's. You could always find her there on her days off. Sometimes I would meet her there and we would shop together and stop at their lunch counter for a bite.

Time passed and Ron, who only worked part-time, was relegated to the Drexel Store in Bexley. I didn't see him much but one time when we were together, he told me a funny story about one evening when he was working in that store.

First, let me give you the lay of the land regarding the Drexel store. We called it the James Road store. In fact, most of the stores were called by their addresses. The James Road store, the Morse Road store, the Kenny Road store, etc.

The store was situated in the heart of Bexley at the corner of James Road and E. Main Street. There was a bus stop in front of the store.

Ron was sitting in a recliner chair near the front of the store reading the newspaper when in walked a lady who was still in her maid's uniform. She stopped in to look while passing time waiting for her bus. The store was small and the entry to the little store was brick with a little step down entering into the showroom. It was only about a three-inch step.

She stepped down and Ron greeted her. He told her to enjoy herself and if she had any questions, he would be right here to answer them. He let her wander as he stayed in his chair.

She meandered through the little store and smiled at Ron on her way out. Little did she know that Ron was paying attention even as he read the paper. He had a full view of the little store.

As soon as she approached the little step up to the door Ron said to her, "Lady, if you can get up that step without breaking the vase between your legs you can have it." And, I might add, Ron tells the story in his gay schtick. I laughed so hard I almost wet my pants hearing him tell this story.

Ron had a lot of friends but no family, so one year I invited him to spend Thanksgiving with my family. There is always a big crowd at our annual Thanksgiving dinners and as usual a bunch of my siblings and their kids attended. About 15 of us were there as I remember. I told the boys I was inviting Ron to our family Thanksgiving and Billy asked me, "Mom, do you think the family would be able to handle this?" I told the boys I didn't care. I never thought of my family as the Archie Bunker type, but I really didn't care. Ron accepted my invitation and he was planning on attending our family Thanksgiving dinner. If they didn't like it, that was their problem.

As I expected, Ron fit right in and was his usual charming self. He is very personable and oh so handsome. He is a master storyteller.

Everything went well. After dinner my family did their usual. They hang around the table and eat more out of the cornucopia fruit and nut bowl and tell the same family stories every year. No one ever gets up to help clean the kitchen and soon Ron came to the table with a dish towel draped over his arm. He put his hand on his hip and said in his very contrived gay voice, "Bea-A-Trice…it's time for us girls to clean the kitchen." Everyone laughed at his theatrical comment but no one was moved enough to help us "girls." Ron poured himself another glass of Boodle's gin and we cleaned the kitchen.

Since Ron was a part-timer with White's, I knew he had a daytime job at Ohio State. So one day I asked him what he did during his full-time job. Again, he was always full of surprises.

He told me he was in pee. I said, "What?" He said, "Pee as in piss." He laughed at my reaction and went on to explain. He had a degree in Chemistry and he tested urine from horses that raced at the Scioto Downs. Oh, well, so much for interesting job descriptions. Ron was a piss tester and part-timer at White's. It was that simple.

The day after Thanksgiving was Black Friday and Gordy had one of his "World's Biggest Sales" advertised in a two-page spread at the Press Journal. I remember Gordy giving me a heads up relating to the merchandise he and our ad man Sam put together in their "double truck" ad. He would ask me if I had any irons in the fire relating to this merchandise so that I could give them a call.

I knew the ad would be an opportunity to have a big weekend on the sales floor no matter how tired I was from preparing the Thanksgiving feast and no matter how un-involved I would be for the kids during the holiday weekend.

My friendship with Joyce was much different than what I shared with Jean and Ron. We were somewhat thrown together because at the time of meeting her we were both Jewish single parents and designers working in the same company. Joyce had two daughters about the same ages as my two sons. She knew the Jewish singles scene in Columbus and dragged me to a few of their dances. We were out one night and she called me in the wee hours of the morning after we got home. She was worried about her teenage daughter who had not come home yet. I told her to go to sleep. She was probably spending the night at her girlfriend's house. I might add, this was all before cell phones.

The next day I got the call. Joyce's daughter was found dead lying in a ditch. It was a suspected murder according to the newspaper article. Joyce was never the same after that tragedy and I don't fault her for that. She retreated from most all social life and did not want any consolation from me. I visited her at home during the mourning period, sat and held her hand, and tried very hard to console her but she kept saying, "It's not fair, it's not fair." I still had my kids and her Laurie was taken from her, she moaned. So sad.

It was hard on all of us who knew Joyce but I realized I must continue my career path. Gordy encouraged me from time to time, to try to break through to her, but it was to no avail. She was never going to be carefree or productive again. I don't think we ever socialized after her daughter's death.

Jean and I continued our friendship both business and personal until I moved to Florida. When I married Steve, the four of us, Jean and her husband Russ, had many enjoyable times together. Russ taught Steve a little about hypnosis and he taught me a little about my golf game.

Tuesdays and Wednesdays were my days off. Sometimes I met Jean at Schottenstein's to shop and have lunch on my days off or you might have found me on the golf course with Russ. They were a wonderful and striking older couple and Steve and I, both being without parents, cherished their friendship.

When I had moments of anger or frustration with my job or my kids or Gordy, Jean was my salvation. She understood and was a calming factor during these moments in my life. I don't think she ever fully approved of the guy I was dating when I met her but as the years passed things changed in that aspect of my life and she met Steve, the guy I finally married. She and her husband loved him and Jean gave her stamp of approval regarding my choice. The four of us, Jean and her husband and Steve and I became close friends.

By the way, not only did Jean dress in shades of beige, her home was decorated in the same monochromatic tones of beiges. It was well done.

CHAPTER 7

ME AND MY MAGAZINES

When I think about reaching my goals as a top designer with little or no formal education in the field, I would be lying if I said I was totally -uneducated in the field. I found ways to educate myself however, there were a lot of obstacles back then and I will briefly mention two.

We did not have cell phones back then and no GPS. I know you are laughing as you read this but really, think about how I found my way to clients' homes with no cell phones and no GPS. On the front of each manilla file where I carefully filled out the client's name, address and phone number on the tab, I also filled out my own GPS. I might as well confess at this time that I have NO sense of direction.

I spent a lot of time on the phone with my client getting directions and I wrote every detail about the directions on the front of my file. If they told me to go east I told them my mind did not recognize east from west. Just tell me if I should turn right or left. So, that's the way I would start with directions. Then they might say go to the four way stop and I would interrupt and ask how far is that from when I took my left turn. They would then say about half a mile. At the four-way stop, you turn right. They would say, you can't miss it, just turn right at the 7-11 store. I would write that on my folder so I could keep an eye out for the 7-11 store. When I reached their street, they would often tell me they were the 12th house on the right.

So, that's a glimpse of the "Bea Gardner GPS system." The other problem was if I was running late or got lost I could not call them on a cell phone because we did not have them at that time in history either. I'd have to find a phone booth and money in my purse to call them. Oh, how easy this part of my job would have been with a GPS on a cell phone telescoped on the screen in my car with Bluetooth.

I got my education in the world of Interior Design from the Bea Gardner School of Self-education. Through my years of art classes, my reading of every shelter magazine I could get my hands on from Better Homes and Gardens, to my collection of the Architectural Digest magazines. I visited every furniture store in the Akron area and I visited the fourth floor of Bloomingdales to view the model rooms that were on display every time I visited or vacationed in the Big Apple.

During the early years of my "self-education," several things stood out. I remember seeing a cocktail table in one of the model rooms at Bloomingdales and I could not get it out of my mind. When I returned to Ohio I visited my favorite furniture experience, Garth Andrews, and talked to a designer there and described the table. He was able to identify the make and model, so I bought it. I think I paid about four or five hundred dollars for the table and today's price for this mid-century used table fetches a $2,200 price tag. It was solid rosewood planking with chrome legs. My experiences and purchases made with Garth Andrews Interior Design Store over the years gave me an extensive background in Contemporary furnishings before I ever got into the business. And I was quite familiar with navigating my way through some of their catalogs while I browsed.

The single most influential person at that early stage of my learning was Barbara D'Arcy. Thanks to her, Bloomingdale's model rooms were the event of the season. Whenever I flew into the Big Apple for a long weekend vacation in the city, the first place I headed for was the 4th floor at Bloomingdales so I could view the model rooms.

She had such a flair for the unconventional. She might pair an orange and purple color scheme that worked where no other designer might go. She was able to throw a flokati rug here, a wicker basket there, and it worked. She made the word "eclectic" a style that was acceptable in the world of design.

One of her best-known showrooms, called "Saturday Generation," was in collaboration with architect Frank Gehry. This room encompassed a warm, monastic feeling by using cardboard as the only material. Very daring, I might say, but I really liked the monochromatic look. In one of my old AD magazines, I went back to that room display over and over again.

One of Barbara D'Arcy's model rooms at Bloomingdale's.
I loved that monochromatic look. Featuring Architect
Frank Gehry's cardboard furniture.

I kept all of my Architectural Digest magazines over the years. In an Architectural Digest Issue May 1978, Fine Interior Design about Barbra Streisand's home stood out as one of my favorites. I remember her line when she said she was "a slave to her tchotchkes."

The hardest part of my education during my road to becoming a "real" designer was learning to scale a room. It was hard for me to admit that I did not know how to use a scale ruler. And math was not my strong suit. And then, all of a sudden, I got it. It was that magic moment when the light bulb went on and I was able to measure a room in inches with my trusty tape measure and then draw that room in ¼ inch scale. Once I learned this important "how to" I was on my way to making professional presentations. I drew most of my rooms on vellum paper and made copies of the room then proceeded to place furniture to scale in the room.

Me in my designer-esque look with my trusty scale ruler in hand. Circa 1982

This was the point in the design job that endeared me to the client. While I was in their home measuring I was conversing casually for clues to their tastes, any pictures that they liked and wanted to keep, talk about favorite colors, and most of all, I was able to find out how the room was to be used.

    I was good at this stage, but I never let the client know. Very often I had the layout of the room completed in my mind and all that was left for me to do was put the room on paper for the presentation. I had a way with my clients at this stage and I usually told them this was a difficult room to do but I would work on it and try to have it done within the next two weeks. We made the appointment for them to come into the store for my presentation. I usually found some quiet time at the store and had the room done on paper within 24 hours of that house call. The rest was fun, picking out colors and fabrics and style of furniture etc.

    Summers were great at White's. I could drive to work with the top down and go water skiing with the boys on my days off. I took my vacations two days at a time on weekends when we had ski tournaments to attend. And, best of all, the boys spent one month or more every summer at a waterski school located in the Hocking Hills in Southern Ohio. Ski school gave my sons life-long friends in the sport and it turned out to be a vacation from parenting for me.

One day I took the boys to the Columbus Aqua Ski Club for a practice session on the slalom course with James. He invited us there specifically to give Bill some slalom lessons and time on the course. Glen and I had a ride through the slalom course too.

When we finished up and were wrapping the ski ropes, my friend James approached me about needing to redo his bedroom and he would like me to help him. He made it very clear that he wanted a designer look and knew that was my area of expertise. I went to his home and measured and we planned for him to come to the store during my slow hours so that we could spend time finding out what exactly he was trying to do with the room. We spent a few weeks at this stage. What style did he like, what color scheme he wanted, and it went on and on. No matter what I suggested he would veto this or that and say, "I think I'll know it when I see it."

I really wanted to do a good job for James but it seemed I was getting nowhere. I finally came up with a plan. I sat down with him in the store and made a suggestion. "James," I said, "why don't you go to the store and buy a few magazines like Better Homes and Gardens and especially Architectural Digest and leaf through them and bring in to me the rooms that you like. I don't care whether it is a bedroom or living room. I just want to see what you like."

It worked. He brought in some pages right out of the magazines with a few looks that he liked. I was able to read into them his tastes and what he was trying to achieve and off to work I went. I used a series of modular campaign style drawers and cabinets from Drexel in an unusual layout and I stayed in a monochromatic color scheme using natural colors. I used textured fabrics to give the room a more masculine look.

Everyone was satisfied. James loved his newly decorated bedroom, and he continued to practice the boys before tournaments behind his Ski Nautique boat. I looked up the Drexel campaign furniture and was surprised to find two pieces that I used in the room. They were fetching a great price on the used furniture market.

One drawer and one chest from the Drexel campaign collection I sold to my client James for about $300.00 per piece and today they will fetch about $2,500 for the two pieces. Mid-century furniture is in demand these days.

Mid Century designs from a good brand like Drexel are in demand. The two pieces I found that I used in his room were going for over $2,500. I think they sold for about three or four hundred dollars each back then. I marked James up as another happy client.

Thinking back on the early years of my career, I not only didn't have GPS or a cell phone, but it was also a time when interior design was not done on computers.

I never did learn the CAD system…Computer Aided Design. I still love to put the pencil to the paper and draw out the furnishings with templates to complete a room. Call me old fashioned, but that's the way it is for me even today.

CHAPTER 8

SOMETIMES IT'S JUST NOT EASY

During the years that I struggled in my career to become a successful designer I also struggled with parenting.

Looking back, I think I was a better employee than I was a good parent. I hardly ever missed a day of work but I sure did miss a lot of parenting responsibilities. Especially at the beginning of my career while I was still a single parent.

Somehow, I managed to attend a few of my son's wrestling matches but I missed most of them. They seemed to be held on my late nights at the store. The end of season potluck awards dinner for the wrestling team was one event that I did not plan on missing but what potluck dinner or dessert could I bring? Cooking something was never going to happen because I had to come straight from work so I had to get creative. I stopped at White Castle on my way to the awards dinner and brought a shopping bag full of White Castle burgers as my contribution.

THE HYBRID DESIGNER • BEA GARDNER

The boys on the wrestling team thought I was the coolest mom because of my potluck contribution. I brought a White Castle bag full of burgers to every wrestling potluck dinner since that first potluck wrestling banquet.

I was working the evening shift at White's when I was paged for a phone call in the late afternoon of my shift. "Hello, this is Bea Gardner" I answered. "Mrs. Gardner" he answered, "Do you have a son named William?" "Yes", I said. The caller was a gentleman from the Whitehall Police Department telling me they had my son in custody. He was caught stealing from a store in the mall and he told me they would keep him detained until I could come to the police station and pick him up.

I got sick to my stomach. I did not go to my manager and tell him I had an emergency and I needed to leave the store. I marched right into Gordy's office in tears and told him about the phone call and told him I had to leave the store. He calmed me down. He spent a few minutes telling me that I was not a bad mother. He told me that his country club friends often have similar problems with their kids. He went on to say that money and time spent with your kids does not necessarily mean they will turn out perfect. Gordy gave me a big hug and sent me on my way to pick up my son at the police station.

Sometimes It's Just Not Easy

As I was driving to the other end of town to pick up Billy, I remembered Gordy telling me rich kids from good families have troubles with their kids too. You're not the only one. They often have kids in counseling for a variety of reasons.

I was still a wreck when I arrived. The policeman at the desk told me they talked to Billy and told me he seemed like a nice young man who had never been in trouble before. All I had to do was sign the release papers and they would turn him over to me. As the policeman turned to go to the holding cell I said, "Whoa. Not so fast. Why don't you go back there and tell him you would not release him to me until he would agree to get counseling. I told the officer I had been contemplating getting counseling for him, however Bill said no. He fought me on that. The policeman said he would not only do that but he told me the counseling would not cost me a cent. They not only got me counseling for Billy, but they also arranged the sessions and a counselor who was well suited for Billy's personality. Whew, I dodged the bullet while doing the right thing for Bill.

So Billy skips school and steals a $10.00 item and gets thrown in jail until I could come pick him up and we never saw the thieves when something got stolen in the furniture stores. Let me explain.

It was a Saturday evening when I was working the late shift in the East store. I did not like working until 9' O'clock on Saturday nights but that's one of the downsides of the retail furniture business. The store was located close to a theater and we got a lot of browsers from couples who were waiting to go to the theater. When you greeted them at the door, they often put their hands up and very defensively said, "we're just looking." In other words, stay away from me. We called them tire kickers.

On this particular Saturday night I greeted two couples who came in together to browse. They seemed like a nice group and they said they were just looking and I kept an eye on them and chatted with them for a few minutes then left them to browse. They told me they just wanted to look while waiting for the movie to start.

Soon I got busy and the last thing I remember about this foursome was seeing them all standing around our DIA chrome and glass dining table. The table was accessorized beautifully with mirrored placemats and Fitz and Floyd beautifully patterned dinnerware with a setting for four. The finishing touches on the well adorned table setting was the gold silverware.

Close to closing time I waltzed past the dining room table and it hit me like a ton of bricks. The silverware was missing. There was no doubt in my mind that the nice-looking foursome were the culprits of the silverware heist. I remember seeing the four of them surrounding the table and could imagine them saying "ready set go." Each one of them probably reached

Sometimes It's Just Not Easy

down and took a place setting and quietly left the store with our beautiful gold silverware. I relayed this scene to Gordy the next day and he was angered. I think it was the first time I ever heard him swear.

When you think of stealing from a retail establishment you might think about how easy it might be to steal a tube of lipstick or some small item. I never thought much about thievery in a furniture store until this happened.

Both of my boys, as well as myself, were competition water skiers. The summers were filled with a lot of ski tournaments throughout the State most weekends during the summer months. How was I going to handle this with my work schedule, I thought? Well, as usual I talked it over with Gordy and asked him if I could take my vacation one day at a time so we could go to ski tournaments. I combined that with working on my usual days off in order to keep the flow at work uninterrupted. That was the summer pattern of my work week and it made for a fun and productive summer both with skiing and with work.

I do remember one ski tournament that I could not attend because it was a fourth of July weekend and I had to work the big sale. I arranged for a ski friend to take the boys to the tournament because it was being held in a nearby Columbus location. I remember a moment during the sale at White's when there was a loud noise coming from the roof. It felt like the roof was going to crumble. Weird I thought. That evening when the boys came home from the tournament, I asked how things went.

Glen was upset. He said the water made him fall during his trick event and he did the proper thing to do in that circumstance. He asked the boat driver and the judges for a re-ride. It was denied. They said look Glen, there is no rough water out there. Of course, I was at work and not at the ski site to advocate for Glen and that was the end of it until we read the article in the paper the next day.

Apparently, there was an earthquake at the very moment when Glen had his 20 seconds on the water for his event. We figured it out and we also figured out why the roof was quaking at the same time while I was at work. Oh well, so much for mother nature keeping Glen from earning a trophy at that tournament.

Seems like I was always in Gordy's office crying with a problem about my kids. This one was a big one and it was not my sons who created the problem, it was their father. It was his weekend to spend with the boys and as we had arranged the drop off in the past I drove them to the Howard Johnson's

Sometimes It's Just Not Easy

in Mansfield, about the halfway point between his home in Akron and ours in Columbus. They had their bags packed and he picked them up as planned and I drove back to Columbus. I was looking forward to a weekend with no responsibilities, just me and my job and what little social life I had, until I got that horrible call from the ex. He told me over the phone he was not planning on returning the kids. He went on to say he was keeping them. No more visitation, he said. They were his kids and he was keeping them.

I didn't sleep that awful Sunday night and the first thing I did on Monday morning was go crying to Gordy about my dilemma. He listened and finally said I needed an attorney. I did not have one I answered. Gordy got on the phone and called up one of his Country Club friends and handed me the phone. I told the lawyer specifics and he then talked to Gordy for a few minutes and I sighed a hopeful sigh. Gordy told me he was the best divorce attorney in Columbus and he agreed to help me.

Two hours later I was back in Gordy's office. His friend, the attorney, called a judge in Akron and the judge talked to my ex and said if the kids were not back in my hands within 24 hours he would be thrown in jail for kidnapping the kids who were in my custody. Gordy said his friend did this pro bono. Problem solved. I often wondered if Gordy paid him or did he really do the job pro-bono for someone he never met. Or, maybe it was a favor to Gordy.

After that incident things went along smoothly for a couple years and you know what that means? It was the Friday night of Bill's high school graduation. Celebrating the end of his high school years. It was during the wee hours of the night when I got a call from the jail. I'm going to cut this short.

Bill was in a terrible car accident. His car was totaled, and by the grace of G-d neither he nor his passenger friend was injured; however the driver of the other vehicle was found to be dead. They had Bill on vehicular homicide. I will not go into any more details regarding this but I will tell you that Saturday morning I called Gordy at home and in my hysterics I told him I would not be coming to work for a while and explained to him what transpired. I told Gordy I needed to get things ironed out. Gordy was kind, sympathetic, worried and very concerned. He told me to take all the time I needed and said he would be there for me if I needed him. He called me at home many times during this ordeal and he offered me money. Whatever you need Bea was the way he put it. I told him I was in touch with an attorney, and I had taken Glen, my younger son, to spend time in Akron with Grandma. I told him I did not need his financial help but thanked him for offering.

It was at about this time that I met Steve and between him and Gordy I was able to keep my sanity and get my little family of Bill, Glen and myself back on track. The other driver had run a red light and Bill was exonerated from any wrongdoing. I went back to work and soon Bill would be off to college.

Reflecting on what I have just put in writing I realize what an important part Gordy played during my single motherhood career years. Without his help and guidance, I would have not been able to handle a lot of what I just wrote about.

As I reflect on those years as a single mother I remember when Gordy told me a lot of families have similar problems raising kids no matter how different the circumstances. Having had the privilege of getting to know Gordy's two sons in the next few years I began to understand a little of where his wisdom came from.

Gordy's two sons had the general makeup of his oldest being a bit like mine and his Andy being a bit like my Glen. They were both in college at the time mine were in high school so perhaps Gordy had already been through some of the parenting that I went through. Whatever the situation he was a rock where I was concerned with his sincere kindness to get me through a lot of what I have just written about.

I remember a conversation I had with Steve after we had been dating for some time. I said, "I don't know how you can tolerate dating a woman with two teenage sons and my crazy work hours." He answered me by saying, "I like your boys and I don't mind your working on the weekends. We can always go out when you get home." Steve and I married and I was no longer a single mother.

CHAPTER 9
DRESS FOR SUCCESS

Gordy was always impeccably dressed, but why not? He owned the store and had the money to do so and a wife who probably helped dress him as so many wives did during that time. How we "dress for success" in a furniture store is no different than any other business. Neat, clean, and well put together is the unsaid rule.

I always knew where I stood in that department. I had very little money but was lucky enough to be young, somewhat petite and looked good in my 'designeresque" appearance. If you had to describe my look you would say I emulated Diane Keaton in the way she dressed in the movie *Manhattan*.

I never gave it much thought and spent very little on my wardrobe. A few nice pairs of slacks and tight-fitting jeans, conservative plain colored silk blouses and a few nice blazers.

Dress for Success

Beige, black and brown were the extent of colors in my wardrobe. In the winter, I wore boots with my pants… ankle boots, high heeled boots and I even had a pair of cool looking cowboy boots. In the summer I often wore three-inch spiked heels to add style to my look. In those days sandals and Birkenstocks were not ever worn in the business world, and especially not sneakers.

I wore very little jewelry with my outfits, however I did accessorize with neckties and scarves. Occasionally I wore a vest with no blazer and most of the time I ran around the furniture store with my jacket off.

My most expensive pair of pants were a pair of Sasson jeans, and I wore them well. Now that I think back on my wardrobe, I was heavy on wearing jeans and light on slacks. That was my designer look and I felt good about it. Now you know how I dressed. As I thought about my personal dress style, I looked around the store and became very conscious of how others were dressing. Some of the men in the store were real schlemiels. No matter what they wore they were not going to ever win the best dressed salesman award. Going against the grain of dress for success, I can't help but mention Kenny. He was the top salesman in the entire company and I think it might be accurate to say he was one of the most sloppily dressed guys at White's. He wore a lot of brown and, as I recall, a very ugly brown and yellow plaid sports coat. He was fat and nothing seemed to fit him well. Not too small but large and baggy clothes as I remember. He had a scraggly beard and he always looked as though he should comb his hair. His nickname amongst us was the Wolfman. If you put a red and white suit on him, he would look like a dark-haired Santa Claus. But I must say, his customers loved him. He had a way with them. He talked about his five kids and sometimes I think he alluded to his customers that he needed the sale to feed those kids.

My mentor and my idol at White's was Jeannie. She was perhaps the second-best salesperson in the company right behind Kenny. She was by far the best dressed person in the entire company. Jean had a style that only a very genteel lady could pull off. As I said earlier, she used no color in her wardrobe. It was beige and I forgot to mention she would occasionally throw in some white with her beige. Jean wore long skirts with silk blouses and huge belts draped over her hips. She always wore many long strands of pearls that hung down to her belt or some other long necklace type of costume jewelry. Every tone on tone of beige and jewelry was so well put together that you would have thought a costume designer dressed her for a photoshoot. The color never varied. Just different shades of beige, from shoes to jewelry, and it always played well with her striking white hair.

The men on the sales floor were a different breed, but mostly very much alike. I called them the Blue Blazer Brigade. Blue blazers with tan colored or grey slacks and different colored shirts with ties. You would have thought that was the end of it but in their blue blazer uniforms they all looked and dressed differently. None of them were preppy looking. That

Dress for Success

much I can recall. Most of them only had one blue blazer and wore it almost every day. Occasionally they had a different sports coat on. My guess is that it was a suit coat worn as a sport coat. Their pants seemed a bit on the sloppy side and the neckties were old and sometimes actually looked dirty.

The Blue Blazer Brigade did indeed make up the bulk of the male salesforce attire but there were some exceptions. Sammy B was a very smart dresser. He was a bit on the heavy side but he wore his clothes well and they seemed to have been tailored to fit his large frame. He always looked like he came out of a GQ catalog.

Robert Porter, one of the store managers, dressed in suits and ties and was as dapper as anyone on the sales floor. He fit the part and was as nice as he was well dressed.

One guy, I'm going to call him Lefty Lou, not only dressed badly but he had body odor, too. He wore clothes that looked like they came from the bargain bin at Goodwill. His shirts were short sleeved polyester that seemed to hold his underarm sweat. I never disliked him but I never wanted to get to know him. I pictured him as a guy who went home after work to a rooming house and ate a TV dinner and watched television the rest of the evening. I often wondered why Gordy kept him on and I later learned he was very dependable and lived close to the store and opened the store for business every day. He also took on the responsibility of tagging any new furniture that hit the sales floor. Yes, he held a key to the store. So, you might say that was the key to his success.

THE HYBRID DESIGNER · BEA GARDNER

I remember Charlie from the Sleep Shop always looked well dressed. He wore a lot of sweater vests with a well pressed white shirt and tie. I remember one of his sweater vests was a red argyle and he looked great dressed like that, casual but professional.

Of course, not to clump my manager Larry into the Blue Blazer Brigade, I must add that when he did wear his blue blazer, he wore it well. He always dressed the part of a well-dressed manager and had a wardrobe that included more than just the blue blazer.

There was a girl named Kathy who came on board as a designer and salesperson. She tried to emulate me in every way possible. She wanted to be like me and she began to wear jeans with a blazer like me. Well, let me elaborate on her dress. She had a big fat butt and she wasn't very attractive and she could not in a million years pull off my dress style on her body. Now, having said all that, I kept my mouth shut regarding her. She was never a threat to me and would never look cool in jeans and a blazer.

At one of our usual Monday morning sales meetings led by Gordy, he was relaying to us what he learned at a seminar while attending the National Home Furnishings Association, of which he was president. The session was called "Dress for Success." He relayed to us the fact that once we learned to "dress for success" our incomes would rise and of course so would the stores bottom line. Gordy was excited to be telling all about this in a very tactful manner.

Dress for Success

He went on for quite some time about what he had learned in that seminar and he never pointed fingers at any of us but he did set up some parameters. I don't remember all of them but I heard him loud and clear when he said there will be no more jeans allowed on the sales floor. I got nervous, very nervous. I could not imagine not wearing my designer jeans and especially since they were the basis for most of my wardrobe. Where was I going to find the money to buy new clothes and pay for alterations for new slacks to fit my short frame? This new dress code was going to be very stressful and expensive for me to adhere to. I slowly walked out of that meeting with a troubled look on my face because we were told we can no longer wear jeans on the sales floor.

As I walked out of the sales meeting I felt a hand on my arm. It was Gordy. He quietly pulled me aside and looked me right in the eye and said in a very soft and understanding voice, "Bea, you can continue to wear jeans on my sales floor. There are just some who cannot pull the look off like you do and I will not stop you from dressing as you do."

I walked away with tears in my eyes and said, "Thank you Gordy."

Speaking about dress for success reminds me of the faux pas I made dressing Glen for Billy's Bar Mitzvah. Bill was dressed in a beautiful three piece suit and tie and I looked very well dressed for the occasion, however, Glen was not satisfied with his attire. Let me explain. At that time leisure suits were all the rage and even though I did not like to see a grown man in a leisure suit I dressed Glen in one. He hated it and to this day he chastises me for dressing him in one for Billy's Bar Mitzvah.

Billy's Bar Mitzvah with Glen and Grandma and Grandpa. Glen in the dreaded leisure suit.

Being a single mom, and especially a single Jewish mom was not always an easy task. My ex stopped paying me child support for about eight months and I was a bit strapped for cash so I worked on Rosh Hashanah, one of the holiest of holy days in the Jewish calendar. One of my co-workers questioned me as to why I was working on this day. I told her G-d would forgive me for working on this day because he knew I did not want to lose the opportunity of enhancing my income to support my family. I did not tell her I was strapped for money. Furthermore, I told Mary, this holiday was a day of atonement. And I told her that I had not sinned this year so I had nothing to atone for. I said to her, "I did not break any of the ten commandments so I am working." She was very religious and did not buy into my reasoning. She asked me if I had ever lusted for a man during this past year and she stopped me in my tracks. I nodded and said, "You win. I guess I have sinned," and with that I left the conversation because I was called to greet the next customer that would walk through our doors.

I am not going to embellish on this however it was about that same time that Glen made the decision he did not want to go to Hebrew school.

We discussed the consequences and Glen made the decision. No Bar Mitzvah for Glen. I was thrilled, I saved money by not paying for a Temple membership and no longer had to figure out how I could take him and pick him up from the added schedule Bar Mitzvah lessons would burden me with.

CHAPTER 10

THE INTERIOR DESIGN SOCIETY

I didn't know anyone who had credentials with the IDS, nor did I know much about it. I was not sure how to become a member of the Interior Design Society so I pecked around a bit and found out you had to take a test and if you passed you would be recognized as a Licensed Interior Designer in the Interior Design Society. I was interested.

I also found out IDS was specifically geared for Interior Designers who were affiliated with the retail furniture Industry. It was a title I yearned for so that I could legitimately call myself an Interior Designer at White's. No one in the company held those initials next to their name, even though there were a few quasi-interior designers who were with White's at that time.

I buddied up with two of White's Interior Designers who had little cubby hole offices in the rear of the store. They were not part of the sales staff and it was hard to figure out what they did or how they got their clients. I guess I did not pay much attention to their MO (mode of operation). In my later years with White's and long after these two designers were gone from the company, I realized they were there to take care of Gordy's accommodation sales.

What's an accommodation sale you might ask? Well, it goes like this. Gordy is on the golf course at the country club with a few of his buddies and one says to Gordy, "My wife and I are planning to furnish our living room. Do you have any good designers at the store?" His buddy goes on to say, "And, I hope you'll give me a good price. Right Gordy?" The next day Gordy would probably call one of the two designers into his office and put them in touch with his golf buddy and the wife.

He would never take me off the floor to play decorator with his pals at the club. He kept me glued to the sales floor and had no idea of my desire to legitimize myself as a designer. I was on my own in my efforts to reach that goal. I was a single parent at that time and I enjoyed the income I got from my sales commissions. I don't think there was much to be gained financially as a licensed designer at White's.

Time passed and getting those initials next to my name became a dim light to my career. I settled for being an in-store designer with an occasional house call. Most of my interior design experience came from what I will call in-store design and that was another genius method of Gordy's in the business.

Gordy had these large 12x18 graph paper tablets printed for the sales staff to use for an in-store sketch of a room while working with a customer. It had the White's logo on the top of each tablet. If a room measured 9X12 you could count off 9 squares on the tablet and then count off 12 squares and draw the rectangle of the room in that manner. It was a way of engaging yourself with the customer so you could help them place the sofa that they were looking for in the room. Sometimes I used the graph tablet to see if the customer could fit a king size mattress in their room or if they had to settle for a queen. That graph tablet was especially useful in laying out the latest rage in contemporary furnishings, the modular sofa which was called a "playpen" sofa.

I went about learning how to utilize the graph paper in my sales pitch by stalking Jean, one of the woman sales associates. She always carried the big sketch pad with her and I was curious to see why.

I also heard that she was one of the top salespersons in the entire company. She was my mentor and my hero right from the beginning and I knew I could learn a lot from her but there was a big obstacle. We did not like each other. So, as I said, I listened in to quite a few of her customer presentations when she was not aware of my presence. Sometimes I faked being on a phone call as I stood nearby and sometimes, I faked looking up a style number on a sales pad so I could get close enough to listen to her sales pitch. I watched and I learned almost as if I were taking a practical course in college about how to be a successful in-store interior designer.

I overheard her doing this kind of quick sketch with her customer one day. At the early stage during her encounter with the customer she got their name and phone number and placed it at the top of the tablet next to the White's logo. That was lesson number one – getting the customers' name and phone number. I took a mental note of that.

Now, getting back to the king size bed question. During her presentation it was decided they go home and get an accurate measurement of the room to find out if the king size bed would fit. I heard the customer ask her for the drawing and they would measure and get back to her. She would not turn over her sketch of the room. She was very gracious and tactful in the way she did it but they did not get her drawing. She said they should bring in the actual measurements and they could redraw the room and that was the end of her "up" with that customer. She handed them her card with the task of coming back with the real measurements and she got back in line for her next up. That was lesson number two. Never give your rough sketches to the customer. Keep it in your files for your return business.

I quickly picked up on the benefits of selling in this sales/design kind of technique. I got really good at it and occasionally it led to a house call so I could measure the customers' room, showing doorways and windows and other things necessary in order to do an accurate scale drawing . I always scheduled my house calls on my days off so that I would not miss out on any sales opportunities during regular business days. These customers were no longer customers, they were now clients. Clients gave me opportunities to do add on sales. In other words, if I were laying out a bedroom set, I might be able to add on the nightstands to the sale and add on two lamps for the nightstands. Every add on increased my commissions.

The more I did this sort of thing the better I got at the nuts and bolts of the design business. I had to teach myself to use a scale ruler and draw the room to ¼ inch scale. I always made many copies of the blank room so I could bubble the room. That is when you draw bubbles for the furniture in the room. A bubble for the bed and dressers and chest of drawers and in the bubble drawing I walked through the room with my pencil to make sure the traffic patterns flowed properly. A lot had to happen before you put your pencil to your blueprint of the room.

Often inches counted in a layout. I loved this part of the design process.

It was about that time that Gordy became president of the NHFA, National Home Furnishings Association. It was a big deal for Gordy and he seemed to step up his game to a higher level in the furniture business, if that were possible.

Gordy approached me one day and asked if I would be interested in becoming a member of the IDS. I don't know if he remembered that I had asked him several years back how I could make that happen. I answered yes and it did not take much time for him to pass the application on to me. I filled out the paperwork, Gordy signed it, and I took the exam and passed with flying colors.

I remember reading the criteria for the room layouts and thoughtfully completing the two floor plans in the allotted time with a proctor in the room. One plan was a two-bedroom residence, and the other was an attorney's office. It was a simple test. The floor plans were already drawn up and all I had to do was furnish the rooms.

I remember having to number each item in the plan and coordinating the individual items by number in the key to the right of the drawing. To me it didn't seem much different than writing a sales slip consisting of a room full of furniture. I passed the exam on the first go around. I became a credentialed Interior Designer. The only problem was I had no office to hang my certificate. Gordy was happy to be able to tell his NHFA friends that he had an IDS certified designer working in his company.

Let me mention that Gordy allowed me to teach interested members of his sales staff how to properly use the White's tablets of graph paper. There were always a few quasi decorators in the group. It was fun. I loved teaching others how to utilize some decorating skills to close the sale.

Becoming a member of the Interior Design Society didn't do anything to better my job situation and here I was, helping all the would-be designers sell from the graph paper tablets.

After I got my IDS certification, I still had to fight for every dime I made by way of my floor sales. It was at that time I decided to move on. I quit White's and moved on to Glick's furniture for greener pastures.

I secured an interview with Mr. Glick, owner of Glick's Furniture. He offered me the job of sales and design with an office of my own in the design studios. It wasn't much more than a cubby hole office with a desk and two chairs. Mr. Glick only asked one thing of me. If they were going to invest in me he made me promise that I would not go back to White's. I agreed and moved into my new job and my new office and took my turns on the sales floor and was content there. The best part of my new job was the location. The Glick's store was located much closer to my home and the long drive to White's Northland store was something I would not miss.

My new position at Glick's was actually a bit of a slap in the face to Gordy for not seeing me as anything but a good salesperson.

At Glick's I got along well with the floor salespeople and the two or three designers who had adjoining offices to mine. The thing I missed most about the change was the fact that the furniture was not the same kind of high-end brands compared to the brands carried by White's. It was like going from selling a Cadillac at White's to a Ford at Glick's. It took a little bit of getting used to.

I became close friends with Shirley, one of the other designers. We would talk about how the design industry frowned on us as designers because we worked in the retail furniture industry. My IDS certification meant nothing to the snooty group of designers because they carried the NCIDQ label. "Pooh pooh pooh on you" is the way they thought about people like Shirley and myself. They did not consider us designers. That changed for me as I will later explain.

Shirley and I made the decision to go for it. We were going to study and test to become a member of the NCIDQ. We each bought "The Bible" for that test, a book called Interior Design and Decoration and began to study for the test. The book was thick, and it was very difficult to discern what they might be asking in the questionnaire part of the test. We studied for months and finally decided we should apply to be tested.

What is NCIDQ?

The National Council for Interior Design Qualification, or the NCIDQ, is one of the most prestigious exams that a person takes to become certified in the interior design industry. The exam is conducted in three parts and has been developed by and is administered by the Council of Interior Design Qualification or the CIDQ. The CIDQ was founded in 1974.

If you did not have your NCIDQ certification it became THEIR law that you were no longer able to call yourself an Interior Designer. You could call yourself a decorator but NOT an Interior Designer. So, Shirley and I studied and studied and finally we felt ready to take the exam. It was about a $600 venture. The test and materials cost about $400 and the test was only administered in Cincinnati which was over 100 miles south of Columbus. That required two nights in a hotel and meals during the testing weekend.

I don't remember much but I do remember you had to pass all three parts of the exam in order to get your license. At that time Steve and I were married and he was an architect. He helped me study. It was almost impossible for me to fail the exam with his tutoring, however I did fail. Shirley and I spent exam weekend together with the knowledge we thought we had passed. She failed too.

Shirley and I decided to study a bit more and we made the trek down to Cincinnati to take the exam again. We both failed again. Steve helped me mark up and understand the reflected ceiling plan and I really thought I was ready this time. I failed the written exam by one point. I was upset. I contacted the board in NY for an explanation. I wanted to know what crucial questions were not answered properly to create this failure.

After some time passed, I got a letter from the testing committee telling me I did not know bedding sizes.

Wow, I thought. If that was the best lie they could give me for the reason I failed their exam I knew I would never be able to test my way into this prestigious society.

It was with this information that I knew that the likes of a retail furniture salesperson like me was never going to be granted membership in ASID. I also learned that most, if not all, designers in the Columbus area who had these initials next to their names never took the test. They were grandfathered in once the testing became a necessity for these initials.

Not passing the test because I was told I did not know bedding sizes made me laugh. Oh well, I knew I was as good or better than most of these snoots, especially regarding bedding sizes.

White's had a whole section of their stores called Sleep Shops. All of Gordy's sales force were experts in bedding and I knew the sizes of every mattress manufactured in the business. We were red carpet dealers with the Simmon's Mattress Co, and I still have my big button from Simmon's that reads, "I Only Sleep with The Best." The excuse for failing me did not pass the smell test in my humble opinion.

Mattress sales were a bonus because as well as the commission from White's, the Simmons sales rep came in once a month and passed out "spiff" money for our bedding sales. He came in with the brown money envelopes and passed out cash to those of us who sold bedding in that particular month. If I sold 5 mattresses in one month $100.00 certainly was a nice bonus.

The Simmons rep gave us this button to wear to enhance our mattress sales. I had a lot of fun with it when I wore it to a singles dance one night.

There were two things I took away with during my venture into ASID. One was that membership in ASID was not ever going to improve my income and number two I began to realize that most of the ASID members were designers who were grandfathered into the Society before there ever was a testing process.

So, I wear my badge that says I only sleep with the best as a badge of courage knowing that they lied. I did know bedding sizes and I have my certificate from the Interior Design Society telling me I was a certified designer to prove it.

CHAPTER 11

TO SELL OR DUST...THAT IS THE QUESTION

    I had the early shift on this particular day, 10 to 6, and I decided to freshen up the Contemporary section of the store. Every section of the store had a different color carpet and the Contemporary section sported a dark brown carpet that showed every piece of lint. My mission that morning was to run the vacuum in the rear of the store. I kind of liked that chore, especially since I knew I would not be getting an "up" for a while. Not only did I get my exercising in, I also could lose myself in my thoughts while running the sweeper.

    I was into the moment when I got a tap on the shoulder. I turned off the vacuum. It was Gordy, and next to him was a stranger to me. A tall, handsome man in a suit and tie. My mind went blank. He was not any rep that I knew. I shut off the sweeper and Gordy proceeded to introduce me to this guy. He said, "Bea, this is my friend Jim Kittle. He owns stores like ours in Indianapolis." He said to his friend Jim, "This is our star in our new Contemporary showcase that I was telling you about." I looked at Gordy then turned my head to Jim Kittle and smiled and said, "I don't know what he's talking about. I am the head cleaning woman in the store." With that I turned on the sweeper and got on with my task of freshening up my area.

I usually arrived at the store about 15 to 20 minutes before opening hours knowing that Lou would have us opened for business at least 45 minutes before anyone else got there. Soon the rest of the employees started to straggle in.

There was a reason for my early arrival. I always wanted to be there early enough so that I could get my name on the "up" list before anyone else beat me to it. By now you probably know that when it's your turn you get to greet the next customer who walks through the door. That will be your customer until they leave the store. Once they leave the store you are then able to put yourself in the lineup for your next "up."

Gordy would have a fit if we all congregated around the front door. It could be very intimidating to the customers, and they might think they were walking into a pack of used car salesmen. When you got your "up," you then paged for "Maggie" line seven. There was no one in the store named Maggie and that page was heard by everyone in the store to alert the next in line for their up. They would then hustle to the front door to greet the next customer who walked through the door.

The sales floor had a diverse bunch of employees and the mix on any given day made it interesting as well as challenging.

To Sell or Dust...That Is The Question

Some of my fellow employees were easier and more fun to work with than others.

Getting there early had a few other benefits. I always looked over the prior day's list of sales to make sure I was not ripped off. Trust me when I tell you this, we all checked out that list. Sometimes one of your customers' names might appear on the list as a split sale meaning that it was your day off and the salesperson who handled the sale split the commission with you. That was fair, but often that was not the case. Sometimes you got ripped off. The "ripper" as I will call them, when accused, will tell you the customer never mentioned your name when they came in. With that excuse the "ripper" would write the whole sale in their name. When your livelihood depended on commission, it quite often became a dog-eat-dog business.

We called ourselves salesmen back then. We were not called saleswomen, nor salespersons...we were just called salesmen. I never called myself a salesman. If I were asked what I did for a living I would just say "I sell furniture" or I would say "I'm in furniture sales." At the early stages of my career, you might say I was a salesperson with a knack for interior design. That's why I called myself "The Hybrid Designer".

I didn't care what you called me as long as you called me Bea. That brings me to a major hazard one faces while working on the sales floor. I was very aware that stealing a customer from one of your fellow workers is commonplace in this business. I did not resort to this kind of behavior. I considered myself to be an ethical person and strong enough to face the challenge of the sales floor without resorting to these tactics. It just wasn't in me.

When I talked to other folks on the floor about Kenny, I was told if he ever takes a sale from you it won't do any good to complain to management because everyone has done so at one time or another. They went on to say, Gordy will never let him go. He was too important to the company's bottom line.

I chose to tackle this potential problem myself because I remember how fast he honed in on my customer on my first day of selling during the warehouse sale. I thought about it long and hard and decided I would try to nip it in the bud with this guy. I confronted Kenny and told him if a customer came in and asked for me, he had better think twice about stealing that customer from me. I made it clear to him that if I caught anyone doing that, I would pay them back in a big way. I said, "If you steal just one sale from me, I will make it my mission to steal 10 customers from you." I went on to say that when he steals a customer from me it would be as though he were stealing money right out of my pocket. I also told him I needed every penny I earned to raise my family because I was a single mom.

I think I scared him into thinking what I might do to him if I were able to steal sales from him with no conscience. He must have thought it over and realized he had a wife and five kids to raise so he decided not to mess with me. We became good friends on the sales floor, and he always called me "BeBe." He was just a big teddy bear. After that, I can't recall ever having any problems working with him. We always talked about our kids and their sports. I talked about my sons and their water-skiing accomplishments and he talked about his kids who played little league baseball. And just like that, he and I became good friends.

Rumor got around that I was not the one you would try to steal a sale from. "Don't mess with Bea" is what they said about me. That is, until a new hire was thrown into the mix on the sales floor. Her name was Lee. It rhymes with Bea. She was a retired schoolteacher and close to my age and short like me. She quickly figured out that to enhance her commission check she could easily steal customers from me because our names sounded the same. If caught she would say that she thought they asked for her in her sweetest schoolteacher voice. I remember going to my manager about her method of pretending to be innocent as she stole customers from me. She would tell him she thought they said Lee not Bea and she thought she sort of remembered them. My manager seemed to think it was a valid mistake on her part. She was not doing this sort of thing intentionally, he would tell me. I had to accept the fact that tattling on her did me no good. I could only depend on the skills I had acquired to endear my customers to me. I told my customers that when they returned to the store and asked for me to make sure it was Bea not Lee and would they please ask for me at the door. I wasn't taking any chances since my manager would not confront her. And, I must say most of my customers were loyal to me so most of the time it was no problem.

A lot of words that start with the letter F come to mind as I think about my job, such as, Fine Furniture, the Furniture Floor, Flurry of customers, Focus, Follow-up, Fellowship, Fashion, Flourish, Fun, Finish, Family and Freshen up.

When I think about Finish, I usually think back to the Thomasville tour and recall our tour guide describing the 24 Finish coats that go into a dining room table. But I also have a Finish story that might have been a disaster for me.

Gordy and gang were off to the furniture market in the Carolina's. I was working on a layout at a desk that was situated in a room setting on the sales floor. I left the desk to check out a fabric number and I also left a lit cigarette in the ashtray. When I came back, the cigarette had rolled off the ashtray and its shape was clearly burned into the desk. I panicked. OMG, I thought. What am I going to do? I pondered the problem and came up with a hopeful solution. I called our service department and told them the problem. I didn't tell them I did it. I let them assume a customer did the damage. Service sent one of their best repair guys over to the store to assess the damage. He didn't ask me if I had been the one smoking and he went about repairing it. He said it will take a bit of time but since it was a solid wood product the repair guy said the job was doable.

He sanded the burn mark and stained and blended the spot to match the existing desktop. He finished the job using

To Sell or Dust...That Is The Question

a fine brush to draw the wood grain onto the damaged area. I have pretty good eyes and it was hard for me to see anything that would make me think there had ever been a burnt imprint of a cigarette on that desktop. Wow, I thought, this guy's good. I think he suspected me to be the culprit, but I was pretty sure he would not tell my manager about this when they all returned from the market. I was right. I dodged the bullet.

I'm on a roll so I'll tell you another F story. The word is "Freshen."

Imagine a 55,000 square foot home. That was the square footage of the Morse Road store. The East store and the Kenny Road store are not far behind in size. The James Road Drexel store in Bexley and the warehouse store on the westside of Columbus added more footage to the White's family of Fine Furniture Stores. We were the "It" furniture store in Columbus. I took pride in saying I worked at White's.

A business of this size needs clean and neat room settings and Gordy's stores were no exception. In fact, we all had sections of the store which were our responsibility to freshen up. Being the cleaning lady for Gordy was what that meant. I never really resented that responsibility, but I must say I never made it a priority in my business day.

On many occasions he would walk through his kingdom and notice little housekeeping things that really set him off. For example, if a lamp cord was showing, or the lampshade had the seam in the front he would rant to whoever was nearby to straighten the shade and hide the cord. In the next breath he would look at the person who was nearby and his whole demeanor changed. He would smile and take a moment to chat while you were turning the shade around. "How are you doing Bea? How are the boys?" And, most often he would say, "Do you have any irons in the fire?" meaning, "Are you working on any big sales at this time?" That was Gordy.

I asked my manager for the section at the front of the store to be mine to keep clean and fresh looking. I wanted to be always guarding the front door to make sure I got my fair share of ups and to make sure I would not get ripped off with one of my be-backs (return customers).

Gordy waltzed into the store one fine morning and I happened to be at the front desk waiting for my up. He seemed to be in a hurry to get to his office and he said a quick hello. He got about five yards further into the store and stopped. He went into a rage about the dust on the dining room table. He went on to rant and rave and said, "Whose area is this?"

I moved closer to him and confessed. I said to him, "I'm sorry Gordy. It is my area to dust." Then, before he could say another word, I slammed the sales slip in my hand on the table and smiled at him. In a very calm voice I said to him, "Would you rather I dust this table or can I finish doing the paperwork on this sale? My customer is coming in shortly with their deposit." Gordy got all red in the face and he stuttered back to me with "Don't worry Bea, I'll dust the table."

I don't recall if Gordy dusted my area that day, but I would not put it past him. I do recall him tactfully telling us in one of our weekly sales meetings that we should all pay more attention to our areas of responsibility. A clean room setting sells better than a messy one, he would say. I just smiled at him as he relayed that tidbit to all of us in the sales meeting.

And to this very day I can't stand to see a lamp cord showing and I absolutely will not tolerate having a lampshade seam visible in the front.

I put Gordon's approach to housekeeping into my personal life. I never gave Billy and Glen an allowance but I paid them for doing chores around the house whenever I had extra money from a big commission check. They would run the sweeper, empty the dishwasher and I definitely taught them how to run the washer and dryer. Yes, they did their own laundry. The main thing I hammered home with them was that during my late nights at White's I did not want to come home to a dirty kitchen. I very rarely told them to clean their rooms. That was their domain. And, as you might guess, Glen's room was neat as a pin and Billy lived in a pigsty. I'd like to think Glen got his neat and tidy habits from living on a submarine while in the Navy, but he was always that way. I don't know where Billy got his messy habits from. It certainly was not me.

CHAPTER 12

CHANGE IS IN THE AIR... THOMAS RUFF

I was getting along famously with my customer and his wife on that uneventful evening at White's. Richard and his wife were looking to furnish their living room, and they decided to do the job properly.

They told me they had raised a brood of kids and the room was heavily used and heavily abused. The kids were all grown and they decided as empty nesters to finally make the room right. We scheduled a house call so I could get measurements. I would blueprint the room to scale. I did not know that this house call would change my life and my career path.

A few weeks after I made that house call, I was ready to give my presentation to Richard and Helen. I might mention, I did not have a design office at White's at that time. According to White's, I was still considered a salesperson and possibly a salesperson and designer. My presentation was set up on the

Change is in the Air...Thomas Ruff

sales floor at a conveniently located dining room table. I cleared off the table and laid out the fabrics and catalogs necessary for my presentation. I chose a dining room table that had the collection of tables I planned on using in their living room, a good "show and tell" approach. After my presentation, I walked my clients around the store to the sofa and loveseat I had selected for them so that they could sit on the furniture. I pointed out a few other things I would be using in the room and all that was left for me to do was convince them why I used the fabric and color scheme as presented. Because I had the room laid out and scaled to size, I was able to show them traffic patterns, etc. Everything went well and Richard and Helen bought the room as presented. We all got along famously.

About one week later, while their newly designed room was in the special-order phase of the sale, I got a call from Richard. He wanted to speak to me and we made an appointment for the next day. I got a queasy feeling in my stomach about the sale. *Oh no,* I thought. Something came up and they either wanted to cancel or change a fabric or something.

Richard came into the store at about 5:30 the next evening during a time when I was not busy, and he started the conversation. He told me he was Vice President of Sales for Thomas Ruff Office Furniture and offered me a job selling office furniture. The conversation was more complex than what I am writing but the outcome was that I decided to take the job.

Thomas Ruff was a Steelcase dealer. I think at that time they were one of the largest Steelcase dealers in the State of

Ohio. I knew nothing about office furnishings and did not know one brand from another. Richard told me not to worry. We will send you to Steelcase school and you will learn everything you need to know about the product.

I was no longer a single mother at that time. I was married to an architect who knew plenty about office furniture, and he encouraged me to consider leaving White's and getting on board with the other aspect of furniture.

Bea and Steve circa 1983. As you can see, I began coloring my hair a beautiful auburn color. No more grey.

On my day off, I drove to Thomas Ruff and I walked through their sales floor and realized that desks and credenzas and file cabinets and modular floor samples seemed like an okay way to go in the furniture business, and I took the job. I would be making more in salary than I ever made in my best years of commission at White's. And the best part of the job was the fact that I would have a real nine to five job. No more working on weekends, no more working during evening hours and no more working on special holidays like 4th of July and New Year's Day. No more retail hours. Wow, I was going to have a real life and still make more money than fighting the fight on the furniture sales floor.

The world of modular furniture cubby holes was new to me. Thomas Ruff wasted no time at all with my training. They sent me to Steelcase school. If I were to become top notch in the business of office furnishings, I had to learn the product and how to sell it. And, how to put it together.

Steelcase school was a highly organized and interesting production. The make-up of students in my class were from many different locations around the country and the world. We had a group of young Chinese students who were going to work in a Steelcase dealership in Hong Kong. Every day after breakfast we got picked up by the Steelcase bus from the Amway Hotel in downtown Grand Rapids, Michigan, that took us to the factory. We juggled most of our time between learning products and about the pieces and parts to assemble the products.

The classes at Steelcase were geared to educate us on everything from soup to nuts about their product. We learned how to read the very large catalogs and we were given a complete packet of Steelcase templates in order to lay out their products in an office setting. We toured the many facets of manufacturing from the upholstery department to the chair factory where the chairs were put together by robots. Most of all, we were being taught to sell and assemble the hundreds of variations of the modular cubby hole offices. It was all very informative and mind boggling at the same time.

Steelcase was very good at breaking up the detailed part of learning their product with bus tours of the town of Grand Rapids. I remember them taking us to a river and watching the salmon swim upstream. That was an interesting sight.

The best tour we had was a detailed tour of the Meyer May home built in 1908 by Frank Lloyd Wright. Steelcase purchased the house in 1985 and meticulously restored its interior and exterior to its original design. The restoration took two years. The restoration had only been completed about one year prior to my class at Steelcase. We were given a tour of the house and the tour guide took us through the entire renovation process. We were shown a video of the painstakingly slow process of removing the layers of wallpaper to get down to the original paper. I loved the tour and all its history that was uncovered regarding the renovation.

Another interesting thing about Steelcase school was getting to know a little about the Chinese kids who were attending. They were twenty somethings learning to make their mark in the business world. I learned a lot about their culture from conversations on the bus ride to and from the hotel and Steelcase. We exchanged business cards and they all had two sided cards. One side was in Chinese and the other side was in English with their "adopted" English name. They had simple English names like Tommy or George or Linda. The back side, or in this case the front side, was their Chinese names and addresses. I asked them to describe their typical living situation at home and they said they lived with their parents in about 600 square feet of living space, mostly in apartments. They told me they did most of their business meetings in restaurants. I described my 2800 square foot, three floor condo at Little Turtle that housed my little family of four and they were shocked. It seemed like a mansion to them and way too much space according to their standards.

Evenings were a hoot during Steelcase school. We had meals and lodging at the Amway Hotel. As I recall, the Amway Hotel took up the better part of two blocks in downtown Grand Rapids. A lot of us gathered in the club/bar/theater in the hotel and enjoyed Tootsie, the big blond bombshell who entertained every night at the Amway. It was a lot of fun.

At the end of Steelcase school, we all were introduced to the Steelcase store and I bought a souvenir to take home with me. I bought a little metal Steelcase truck in the Steelcase store.

Now that I look back on my days at Thomas Ruff, I remember things like this more than what I learned during Steelcase school.

The little toy truck was 9" long.

I went back to Ruff's with a vague, if not a little better, degree of knowledge about selling office furnishings and using the Steelcase catalogs. It was now time to dig in and be a part of the salesforce. Little jobs were pushed my way through my friend Richard. He mentored me and helped me do the pricing part of the sale which was a lesson in math that was a challenge all of its own. None of it came easy for me. I was used to the floor sales method of pricing out a sale from a retail point of view and Ruff's sales quotes were an animal of a different color. It was not easy for me, and I was grateful my friend Richard could walk me through all of this with a whole lot of patience.

Richard liked me and felt responsible for bringing me on board and I was thankful for his help and understanding. I slowly evolved and learned a bit of what the designers in the company did and I can honestly say it was not for me. The designing part I mean. It was all computerized. They had a specialized staff who could do 3D drawings on the computer and change product color at the click of the mouse. I was brought in because of my people skills and sales acumen, not as a computer designer.

If I were to get involved in a potentially large job like many floors of an office that would include individual offices like sales manager to a VP office and then many repetitive floors of modules, Richard would immediately assign the job over to someone in a more seasoned sales position than I. Someone on the sales staff who knew what they were doing. That salesperson would then work hand in hand with the design staff who set things up on the computers and were then able to give the clients a 3D color presentation so they could see the space set up. It was no longer my client. I only got credit for the initial encounter and turnover with the clients.

I found these sales with little or no continued client contact very unsettling and I also found the design aspect of commercial design very unsatisfying. I can only describe it in this manner. If I were decorating a high-rise office building such as Nationwide Insurance, I might do the initial layout with a grass cloth wall covering and then just multiply that part of the sale by the square feet to include 17 floors of grasscloth wallcovering. Nope, this whole sales/design scene was not for me. Too boring.

At Ruff's, one of the salespersons had to come downstairs when they were scheduled for floor duty. They all hated that part of their job. They needed to be upstairs at their computers figuring quotes and product for sales in progress. Floor duty stopped them from doing that when they were assigned to babysit the showroom floor about every ten days or so. But I loved floor duty. It made me think of White's and I enjoyed the challenge of waiting on a customer who walked in on a more personal level.

My friend Richard was astute and realized this part of my sales persona. He took the bull by the horns and got with Jack, the owner of the company, and created a position for me as manager of the retail showroom. I was to greet the clients and find out what they were hoping to accomplish with our company. If it were just a showroom type sale, such as an accountant's office or a doctor's office and waiting room or even a home office, I was in my element. In this capacity, I felt as though I were back at White's.

Not only was I the showroom manager, I was also considered to be an ambassador who was able to qualify the walk-in customer who needed to be funneled upstairs to the "real" sales staff. My position was a win-win for everyone and I fell into this new position very well. I kept the showroom in tip top condition, funneled a few big jobs upstairs, but in the end, I got caught up in a power struggle between my friend Richard and the owner's brother. His name was Bob.

Bob did not like me very much, especially since I was brought on by his rival, Richard. He especially did not think my position was warranted. In order to save money for the company, he wanted to go back to the old way of having the sales staff do floor duty and do away with my position. One slow morning, Bob walked into the store and found me at my desk reading the newspaper. He walked over to my desk and got nasty with me, accusing me of being lazy and sitting around reading newspapers on the job. He screamed this at me.

Right about the time this incident happened and I was ready to throw in the towel, I got sick. I found out I needed a hysterectomy and Thomas Ruff very kindly allowed me the six weeks off for surgery and recovery and paid me during that process. What a deal. At White's that would not have happened. So, when I was able, I went back to work at Thomas Ruff.

But I knew after the confrontation with Bob, it was all over for me at Ruff's. Bob's temper tantrum and his treatment of me in that situation was the end of my 18-month experiment in the office furnishings business.

I called my old friend Gordy and said, "Hi Gordy. This is Bea. Can I have my old job back?"

CHAPTER 13

PEPTO BISMOL PINK

By this time in my career, my name was recognized as a designer in Columbus amongst other designers in town. Now mind you that was not always in a good way. The snooty design community looked down upon any designer who was affiliated with a retail furniture store. It didn't matter what my credentials were, nor did it matter who my clients were. It was a stigma to be an interior designer affiliated with a retail business.

The only designer I knew who rose above that stigma was a fellow from Centners named Mark. He had a great reputation and Centners also had a reputation for being the only store in town that hired real designers. They were not dual credentialed – sales and design as was I.

At one point I decided to inquire about a job with Centners. I got an interview with the owner's husband who ran the business side of the store. We interviewed for about an hour. He told me one of the keys to their success as a design studio store was their secret formula.

"Wow, what was that?" I asked. He told me that each design client had to sign a contract with them that the room would not be delivered and set up until every item specified in the sale was in stock and ready for delivery. And the client was not allowed to be home during the set up. That gave the delivery department and the designer the ability to put the merchandise in place all at the same time whether it was a floor sample or a special order. Pictures were hung, lamps were lit, toss pillows were fluffed. The room was completed right down to the decorative ashtrays if you get my point. When the client entered the newly completed room the wow factor was there, and they signed and approved the entire room full of new merchandise.

He went on to tell me that when a client could see the completed room, they were not looking for flaws in the merchandise. For instance, at White's, a skirted sofa might come in with a wrinkle in one of the pleats, or a striped fabric might not have lined up perfectly. At a delivery from White's, the customer might have complained about these minor things and sent the sofa back. In such a case the service department had to correct flaws in order not to lose the sale. When the room was delivered in total these kinds of things were never noticed by the customer, as was the case with Centners.

I was called a few days after my interview and was told I would not be hired by Centners. I was disappointed and asked why. Mr. Centner (not his real name) told me that he knew

I was good at what I did and could certainly be a success in their operation, however, his wife informed him that I would be in direct competition with her, and she would not be able to tolerate that. Wow, what a compliment and a slap in the face at the same time. The only person that benefited from my not getting that job was Gordy. He never knew of my interview with them.

Shortly after that interview I took a leap of faith. I resigned from White's and took a stab at being in business for myself.

I was chugging along, finding my stride in my own business by now. You could find me in the phone book under Bea Gardner Interiors. A very well-known developer from Cleveland was building a couple models in Columbus and I was operating out of my own studio at the time. The job would be welcome because I was lean on cash at that time. I insisted on a 50% deposit as was the standard in the business for special orders and I was on my way to feeling a little less strapped for cash. I had a few other little jobs in progress at the time, so I was not worried.

After the models were completed, I set about getting paid. They put me off and put me off and by this time I really needed the money. After many phone calls to try to get them to the table to pay for the job, I was getting to the end of my rope.

Pepto Bismol Pink

I had some guy friends at that time and I was telling them about my not being able to collect what was due on this job and one other completed job where I was having trouble collecting. The other job was a well-known restaurant owner. He owed me money after I finished decorating his condo. My friend Denny stepped in during the conversation and told me he would handle these two collections for me. He met up with the restaurant guy, flexed his muscles, and said, "I'm here for the decorator. She wants her money." My client paid up. Then he went to the builder. The builder told him he would meet me halfway at the Howard Johnsons in Mansfield and would have a check for me. Yes, I had my very own collection agency.

I drove my rented white Lincoln Continental to the meet up spot and as planned the builder was waiting inside for me. He gave me a check for half of what he owed me and I balked at that. I told him I had two kids to feed and certainly being part of one of the richest families in Cleveland he could afford to pay me. He answered me with this. He said, "I saw you pull up in a Lincoln Mark V and it looks to me that you can afford to wait." I knew then he would never pay me in full. He was a nasty rich guy that was probably in the habit of stiffing his creditors.

I drove the 60 miles back to Columbus and wasted no time with my next phone call.

I called Gordy and said, "I need a job." He asked, "When do you want to start?" Without hesitation I answered back with one word. "Tomorrow". And that was the end of Bea Gardner, Interiors.

I thought about Centners' secret formula over the years and knew that White's approach to delivering special order merchandise one item at a time as they came in was not necessarily the way to do a whole room. I was blessed with the opportunity, on rare occasions, to deliver the whole set up when I was doing a model home where there was no client involved. All the public saw was a completed room.

To use that philosophy of a completed room setting being set up at one time made for a beautiful visual. I remember decorating a model home for the parade of homes. The builder was a well-known builder and a friend of Gordy's so I was given the job on a silver platter. After my initial presentation, the builder turned the model over for completion to his son. I worked with his son on selection of paint colors with their painter and was sent to a tile source to pick out the bathroom and kitchen tiles within the builder budget and did the selection of cabinetry, lighting fixtures and carpet with the builder's suppliers. Pretty standard process that goes into a typical builder model.

Of course, we were all on a tight schedule to have the house completed by the time the Parade of Homes opened to the public. And to make matters even more time critical for me, I had to complete the home on time because I was leaving for a cruise the day the parade began.

I went to the model to check on things about two weeks before delivery from White's and the nightmare began. They put in the wrong color tiles in the master bath. OMG. I selected a dusty rose tile to go along with the color scheme and when

Pepto Bismol Pink

I looked at the bathroom the tiles were a Pepto Bismol pink. It almost blinded me and there was no way I could live with that color in the master bathroom. All I could think about was my name and picture on the stand-up frame as you entered the home and I'd be known as the Pepto Bismol Pink Girl. It read, *This home has been tastefully furnished by White's Fine Furnishings…Bea Gardner, Interior Designer*. I could not have my name associated with those Pepto Bismol tiles.

I got hold of the builder's son and ranted about the wrong color tile and said I could not accept it. That color was wrong, and it ruined the whole professional look I had achieved. I said to that young whippersnapper he had to contact the tile company and have them tear out this horrible color and install new tiles that I had originally selected. I told him they made a mistake. My nightmare got worse. The young lad told me he changed the tile color because he thought the tile I had selected was dull and he liked the brighter tile. That set me off even more.

Here's what I told him after I calmed down. I said, "If that tile is not replaced with my original selection, I will not deliver one stick of furniture for this model. You will be the only home in the Parade that has an unfurnished home to show. Have it your way, young man." I went on to say I did not want my name on that job.

The tile got changed and the painters were still painting the living room the day before opening. I was at the model pulling the sofa away from the wall for the painters to finish.

The job ended up being completed for the opening and I went home and packed for our cruise.

Gordy asked how things went and told me to have a nice vacation. I smiled and told him the job went well and thanks, I'm looking forward to the cruise. I never told him about the tile. I also never worked for that builder again.

With Bill home for the summer from college and Darren visiting his mom in Jersey and Glen at wrestling camp, Steve and I sailed the British Virgin Islands. Things were quiet on the home front.

When I got back to the store after the cruise, things were not so calm. Back on the sales floor sporting my tan from the cruise, I visited another set up from another builder. I decorated the clubhouse in their newest condominium complex. The condos were upscale in a very upscale neighborhood, and they wanted the clubhouse to make that kind of statement. I worked with Gordy so that I could give them special pricing. The only thing Gordy wanted from the job was free advertising. I pressed on and did a beautiful job for the client. I even went so far as to have the condo logo sculpted into the rug in the foyer.

My clients were very impressed, and Gordy had our advertising firm make up a framed picture of me and the usual verbiage: Furnished and designed by White's Fine Furniture…Bea Gardner, Interior Designer. Everyone was happy until I went to check on the job shortly after the cruise. Our sign advertising White's and me as the designer was taken down. I found out that the builder's wife removed our sign and took full credit for the decorating of the model. She trashed our sign. So much for professional thievery.

You would have thought I learned my lesson about doing business with builders, but I did not.

CHAPTER 14

UFOS & SATISFIED CUSTOMERS

I saw a UFO. I know, it sounds like I'm a bit loony when I admit it but this is how it happened.

I was driving late one night and I had just turned on Winchester Pike. I had about a one-mile drive on that dark, unlit road before I had to make a left turn and an immediate right turn into the little street where I lived.

I saw lights from above following me. At first, I thought it was a helicopter hovering, but it was so quiet that I got a bit edgy. I kept driving and the lights kept following me. The lay of the land was nothing but a large cornfield to my left and a couple farmhouses to my right. In fact, my son's best friend lived in one of the farmhouses.

OK. Back to my story. I kept driving and watching the lights shining down on me. I got to the stop sign at the end of that long, dark road and I turned my head to the left to make sure no cars were coming. As I began to make my turn, I froze. Not 50 feet away from me was this huge flying saucer hovering in the cornfield. Honestly, I'm not making this up.

It was shaped exactly as you have seen them in comic books. This huge object was quietly hovering in the cornfield with a circle of red and green lights in the middle of the saucer shape. As I said, I froze. I was petrified and I finally made a mad dash for home. As I quickly turned left, I stole a look one more time and it quietly just took off and disappeared. I was shaking when I got out of the car and could hardly put the key in the door to let myself in. I very rarely told anyone of this incident because they would think me to be crazy.

Two years later, my UFO sighting would endear me to a client.

I began noticing that Gordy was throwing a few of his country club friends my way. He would always give me a little history of who and what I was getting into before I got involved with them. By the way, Gordy was a board member of the Limited and the owner of the Limited was one of his closest friends. It was no wonder that some of the business Gordy was sending my way were employees of the Limited.

He informed me that one of the Limited big shots was decorating their new home and he offered them White's best designer to help with the furnishings. That did not entice this VP, and he told Gordy that they were utilizing the services of a designer from Chicago and they would not be needing Gordy's help. Gordy must have been insistent so they finally capitulated and allowed Gordy's best designer, that would be me according to Gordy, step in and decorate the three childrens rooms. I finally called the client for my presentation of the three bedrooms. I knew there was a snobbish attitude against using me instead of their Chicago designer for the kids' rooms. Gordy even mentioned to me that they thought White's furniture was not up to their standards. I knew he was hoping I could use my magic to win them over.

Several weeks passed since I was in their home measuring the rooms and I made sure the little cubby hole office was available for my presentation. I did not want to make the presentation on the sales floor as was my usual "office." I was ready.

I tried to make them as comfortable as I could knowing that the mister was not interested in what I had to say. I went to work presenting the son's bedroom first. The mister stood in the doorway with his arms folded. He kept quiet through most of the presentation and seemed a bit disinterested.

I did one room at a time. I presented each layout with the kid's names on the individual drawings. I described the quality of the furniture with pictures from the catalogs and laid out the fabrics and furniture pictures for each room. I went into the color scheme of each room where I was planning to use custom bed coverings and window treatments and left a little wiggle room to add the personality differences of the children into each room design. Diana made me aware of some of what the kids' likes and dislikes were while I was measuring the rooms.

UFOs & Satisfied Customers

    I was very close to finishing the last room presentation when the mister interrupted me and spoke. He said he came to see my presentation expecting not to like what I did and with a smile on his face he told me I nailed it. He was pleased and said to press on and told me to work with Diana to completion. Wow, I thought. Gordy will be pleased.

    Diana and I worked very closely with the selection of fabrics and window treatments while the furniture was on order. She would come into my little office and we would spend about five minutes talking about the kids' rooms and then we would spend the better part of the hour just talking and enjoying each other's company. It was during one of those chats that I found out that she and the mister, and two friends they were out with one night, saw a UFO! I don't know who brought up the subject first but we started describing our encounter and the description of the object and what we described was identical in nature. The most interesting thing to me was that they saw theirs with another couple, so it definitely was not a figment of the imagination. She told me they were walking along the beach at Lake Erie with this other couple after dinner when they spotted the UFO.

    I am convinced that sharing the experience we both had with a UFO made us friends for life. From that time on she did not come to my office empty handed. She would bring me a big green trash bag full of brand-new Limited clothes that just happened to be my size. To her it was like bringing me a bag of candy as though she worked in a candy store. The kids' rooms were completed shortly before the Christmas holiday, and everyone was satisfied. Diana stopped by White's one day during that holiday season and gave me a Christmas card and said inside there was a little gift for my boys inside. I opened it and found a beautiful card and $150. What a wonderful experience it was to work with her and her big shot husband. Diana was a beautiful woman inside and out and very generous.

I was used to juggling a few design clients at various stages of their rooms along with my ongoing dedication to floor sales. It made my job very interesting. In fact, floor sales were where I picked up most of my house calls that led to design jobs. Most of my clients were just average people with average incomes and average homes. During that same period of time when I was working with the big shot VP and his lovely wife Diana, I had another client that was giving me fits over a color I had recommended for their living room walls.

Somehow, I knew that painting the walls in the same background color as the chintz fabric on the sofa was the key to bringing their little living room up a notch or two. The off-white walls were not going to get it, in my opinion. My clients fought me on the gunmetal gray walls I was proposing and just couldn't agree with me on that color. In my mind, that was the only way to go to make the room the high style that

I was trying to achieve. Finally, I told them to please go with the paint sample I was suggesting and if, after the room was complete, they still did not like the color, I would come over to their house on my day off and personally help them paint over that color and turn the room back to the off white walls. I knew once they saw the room put together, they would see things as I did and sure enough, it turned out they loved it. The new color of walls made an average room look high-style and another design job was completed with a satisfied customer.

There were so many interesting clients/customers that I came in contact with during my years with White's. I'll never forget my friend Arline. She was never a design client, just a customer I met on the sales floor. She had a witty, sarcastic, and typical New York personality. She never got into what she called "the white bread" community of Columbus. Occasionally she would come dancing into the store with her I "heart" New York t-shirt on just to gab with me. One day we were talking about bagels and she told me there was not a good bagel to be found in Columbus. She went on to brag about New York "water" bagels. I told her I didn't know the difference between a water bagel and any other bagel.

Arline wanted me to meet her mother who was coming to visit. Sure enough, she waltzed in with her mother and gave me a shopping bag full of water bagels fresh off the plane from New York. She had her mother bring them on the plane and stopped in to give me the bagels before they even went to her home. That's how I met Arline's mother.

Her husband then got transferred to Chicago, and Arline and I continued our friendship.

She was much happier living in Chicago. Columbus, Ohio did not suit her personality.

One day I was talking to Arline on the phone, (pre cell phones and we had long distance charges) and I was uptight and complaining to her about something regarding my kids and I said to her, "I wish I could run away from home."

She didn't miss a beat. She asked me to drop everything and come to Chicago for a weekend. I did. I sent the kids up to Akron for this long weekend and off I went to Chicago. Arline and I went to the Merchandise Mart and had a ball looking at all the furniture. We had a really funny moment when we decided to visit the Pace showroom at the end of the hall we were on. So, we meandered down the long hall talking and laughing and Arline walked straight into the clean and shiny glass door not realizing it was closed. She bumped her forehead and dropped her purse, and at the same time this cute little guy came at us and shouted, "Why don't you watch where you're going lady?" We both started to laugh so hard at the whole thing and he didn't appreciate us at all. We all got over it and checked out the showroom knowing we would never be buying anything from them.

She and her husband, Bob, took me to the Palmer House for a dinner show featuring Tony Bennett that evening. We told Bob our funny story about his wife trying to walk through a glass door. We laughed again. Bob's office was across the hall from Paul Harvey's, and he introduced him to me.

I felt carefree the entire weekend. I came home energized and most of my troubles seemed to have melted away. Just what the doctor ordered. A weekend away from the boys and White's and everything else that was bothering me.

Shortly after my weekend in Chicago, I decided to leave White's. It was time for a change. It was about this time that I took the job with Glick's.

CHAPTER 15

BACK AT WHITE'S AND BEA GOES GREEK

There was a time when I experimented with other furniture stores in Columbus. Mostly because I would get disgusted with something at White's. Either I was not making enough money or I was unhappy with getting nowhere, or sometimes it was just a matter of thinking the grass was greener at another company.

I remember interviewing with Bob Glick, owner of Glick's Furniture Store. Glick's was a large operation similar in size and scope to White's but a notch below in brands of furniture. I knew Gordon was never going to give me my due as a designer. He was always going to keep me as a floor salesperson because that is where he got the most value from me as an employee. I wanted to move on with my design career and Bob Glick offered me a design office of my own as well as floor sales. I had accepted myself as a hybrid designer…as

Back at White's and Bea Goes Greek

equal in sales as in design so this position with Glick's seemed to fit the bill.

Gordon was not willing to give me that. I figured out while interviewing with Glick's that Gordy probably bragged on me over cocktails at the Country Club. Bob Glick as much as said so. Bob Glick told me he would hire me if I promised not to go back to White's. He thought I would go back to White's if Gordy asked me to come back. Hmm. I hesitated and did, in fact, agree to that. I told him I had gone as far as I could go at White's and I was willing to come on as a designer with him knowing that most of my income would still come from floor sales. I was happy there.

I remember giving a design presentation one evening in my little office only to later realize that George, a very well-known designer in town whose office abutted mine, was listening in to my presentation. The next day George approached me and told me that he listened to my presentation and told me that he had become aware of what a good designer I was. He did ask me if I would take a word of advice from him. Knowing he was well respected in the design community and a seasoned designer I said of course I would listen to his advice.

Now, here's what he said: "Bea, the only thing I would do differently if I were you would be to use a long cigarette holder and wear a boa around your neck." I smiled and wholeheartedly took his critique as a very big compliment. George and I got along famously after that. When it wasn't my up, I would hang around his office and in doing so I learned a lot.

THE HYBRID DESIGNER • BEA GARDNER

I was surprised how much I enjoyed all the people I worked with at Glick's and loved getting to know all these characters. The highest paid salesperson on the floor was a lady named Crystal. She was a dynamo...could sell ice to an Eskimo. I overheard her one day saying to her customer, "The color almost matches." And they bought it. I could never imagine myself telling someone the color "almost" matches.

There is no such thing as an almost match. That was the reason furniture salespersons got a bad rap in the design community. They were either salespeople or designers. The fact that I was good at both sales and design was always a problem for me. I liked the whole picture in the furniture business and Gordy understood that part of me. He just didn't know how to focus on what exactly to do with me to keep me happy at White's.

I had been at Glick's for about a year and out of the blue I got paged one evening for a call. I picked up the phone and the person on the other end was Gordy. He went through the formalities. Hope you are doing well and how are the boys and slid right into the reason for the call. He wanted me to come back to White's. He didn't mince words.

He told me I could have the big office next to Tillie's office and that I could design the office and furnish it anyway I wanted. He said he would give me a salary plus a small percentage of commission. Gordy asked me on the phone to stop in to see him and we could talk further. I told him I would think about it and get back to him.

Back at White's and Bea Goes Greek

I did think about it and I must say I thought about nothing else during the next week. Did he really mean I would be getting a large design office and a salary and the business card with the title of Bea Gardner, corporate designer for White's Fine Furniture? Was this really happening to me? To work in that capacity with the man that I admired and in the company that I loved?

I called Gordy back about a week after his phone call and we sat down and ironed out the details of this new position that was being created for me.

Bob Glick was right. I left and went back to White's.

It didn't take long for me to design and furnish my new office. I made it very "presentation" friendly. I kept the long countertop and had cork installed above the counter. I was able to spread out carpets, fabrics and catalogs and pin wallpaper and paint samples and furniture collections on the cork wall. The clients could sit facing everything as I walked them through the entire presentation without having to fumble around juggling catalogs and everything else around a tiny office.

And it didn't take Gordy long to introduce me to the idea of decorating two fraternity houses on Ohio State's campus.

I remember how perfect that office was when I was doing these Fraternity houses. I did them both at the same time.

THE HYBRID DESIGNER · BEA GARDNER

Three handsome alumni men came to me with pictures of what their fraternity house looked like when they were attending college twenty years ago. They had raised funds to decorate and re-furnish the house and they wanted it to resemble what it looked like when they were there. I got a pretty good mental picture of the kind of look they were wanting me to achieve. They had one request regarding my finished product. They wanted the current composite picture to be hanging on the same wall location they had theirs hanging. They showed me a picture of it. I got to work and set about measuring the frat house in order to blueprint the common area to be designed and furnished.

A few weeks later I called them in for the presentation. I had things spread out on the counter and pictures of the furnishings and paint samples pinned to the cork wall and everything was showcased when they walked into my office. The young kid who was president of the fraternity at that time was also included in the presentation. One of the banker type alumni guys was about 6'4" and my being as short as I am, I gave him a chair and kidded with him that he must sit because I could then look him in the eye as I was standing and talking. We all got a laugh and broke the ice. I went on with my presentation.

I used a commercial grade of carpet in a very masculine navy blue and brown plaid and a pair of brown leather Chesterfield sofas. Two wing chairs in a small print and brass lamps on the tables next to the chairs. I picked out two different tones of beige paint colors, the darker beige to be painted

Back at White's and Bea Goes Greek

on the lower half of the chair rail and the upper half would be painted in the lighter color. I pointed out where I would hang the composite over the piano and I thought everything was perfect during my presentation.

They were all nodding with approval and to my surprise the young kid, the president of the fraternity, said he did not like the color scheme. Since I knew I was right on with the entire overall scheme and colors, his comment about not liking the colors through me for a loop. For a moment I was at a loss for words.

Finally, I looked at the kid with a smile on my face, and in a soft voice I said, "Hey, anyone who wears a faded red ball cap backwards, and a purple jacket with brown pants and holes in his tennis shoes has no business not liking my color scheme." And I continued to discuss the pricing of the entire room, piece by piece so that we could finalize the deal. I went on to explain an estimated special-order timeline and went on to say they could get the house painted and cleaned up during that period. I got their approval and told the alumni group of men that I would have the paperwork in order soon for signatures along with their deposits. Whew, got through that one.

As I said earlier, I was doing two fraternity houses at the same time. The one I spoke of was a bunch of beer drinkers compared to a real nice gentlemanly group of young men in the other frat house. I don't remember how I got involved with two fraternity houses at the same time, but it was interesting.

Delivery and set up for both these jobs were as though I was on two different planets. Let's take the brown and blue job first. I arrived about two hours before the White's delivery truck and wouldn't you know, the guys had a beer party the night before. The room was a pigsty, and I quickly gathered a group of the frat boys who were hanging around and put them to work to clean up and get ready for the delivery. They were not happy with me but I was firm. I got nervous when I saw the composite hanging on the wall. It was not a picture with a lot of boys on it. It was a picture with a lot of girls on it. Yes, you guessed it. The composite picture was from a sorority. Apparently, it was the fad in the "Greek world" on campus to steal a composite and put one in its place that did not belong to that particular fraternity or sorority.

Luckily for me I recognized the name of one of the sorority girls in the picture. She was the daughter of a friend of mine. I contacted my friend and he put me in touch with his daughter who helped me to locate the composite I was looking for and I got everything done in time for the dedication of the newly decorated frat house. Whew, I said to myself.

When I got back to the store after a grueling afternoon setting up the first of the two frat houses, Gordy asked how it went. I just rolled my eyes and with no further discussion said, "Job done."

The second set up on house #2 was a dream come true for any designer. The boys were there to help me. They set up and plugged in the lamps, helped me to move the furniture a little this way and a little that way and were very appreciative of everything I did. The crowning glory of that job was

Back at White's and Bea Goes Greek

the beautiful round rug in the foyer. I had the fraternity logo sculpted into the rug. It was a work of art and set the pace for a job well done. Everyone was happy.

These two jobs came shortly after I came back to work for White's, and I feel certain Gordy brought me back to get me involved with these two frat houses. I imagined he figured I was the one person he knew who could handle both jobs. Though he was correct knowing I could handle these jobs, I prayed I would never have an opportunity to do anything with the Greek community on any campus ever again.

I never told Gordy about my having to hunt down the composite picture and I never mentioned the 12:30 am phone call from a bunch of drunk pledges about which half of the walls get painted the light color and which half gets painted the dark beige even though I had the walls marked.

Welcome to my world.

A few years later I never dreamed my son would go Greek but he did. He visited the Jewish fraternity and decided Greek life was not for him and as he was walking back to his dorm he was called into another frat house for a peek and really liked the guys there. Yep, he went Greek.

Bill was the only Jewish guy in the fraternity and on several occasions, he was addressed as the "Jew Boy." He changed that. During his second year he placed himself into the role of pledge master and he recruited four other Jewish boys into his fraternity and that seemed to stop the "Jew Boy" salutations. But I will tell you that his fraternity house was more like the first one I decorated. On Mother's Weekend, I found out they were a bunch of beer drinking, party going guys who seemed not to have a neat bone in their bodies.

CHAPTER 16

THURBER HOUSE

Straight up the narrow steps and a sharp left turn into the attic apartment. That is how delivery of the furnishings had to happen in this writer's apartment. Our delivery guys got the beautiful country french style desk with the leather insert up the stairs and into the apartment legs first and at an angle. Next came the sofa. These guys were good, I thought. They carried the sofa up the steps by the legs and back so it could clear the narrow steps, and when they tried to lower it a bit to make the turn into the room…it got stuck. About another 10 or 15 minutes later and after leaning and tilting the sofa in all directions, it was apparent that it would not fit. I watched what was happening and I said, "Let's get a hammer and knock out part of the drywall ceiling." I finished the set up and knew that I had to give Luke Feck a call and confess to putting a hole in the ceiling.

THE HYBRID DESIGNER · BEA GARDNER

Luke Feck, Editor of the Columbus Dispatch, headed up the renovation of the Thurber House and as part of the renovation, the attic space was going to become a residency for a talented author. The residency allows the author to focus on his/her own project(s) and is designed to provide a writer with the gift of time to develop a work in progress.

Gordy was invited to participate and asked to furnish the third-floor apartment of the Thurber House in Columbus, Ohio so it should be no surprise that he asked me to head up that project. Gordy and I discussed the best way to handle this and we decided to include the other major furniture stores in town to co-op with us. I set about contacting Bob Glick and others in the business for donations per my drawing of how the apartment would be laid out. White's donated the desk from a Pennsylvania House collection and I managed to get the other furnishings donated. Scheduling delivery and set up was the biggest challenge and I managed to get the job done by the time the newly refurbished museum was completed.

I called Feck after the delivery and asked him to come to the site and view the space when I completed the job. I said there was a slight problem and I wanted him to see it and could he come asap. I did not want to explain my delivery nightmare over the phone. He met me at the apartment and I showed him the damaged ceiling that I had to knock out and went through the gyrations of how we had to make the delivery of the sofa to get it in the room. He had a little smile on his face as he watched my animation of the explanation of why I had to ruin the drywall. He was gracious and said, "No problem, I'll get the drywall crew back to repair this ceiling immediately." It was done and the grand opening of the museum went as planned.

It makes you wonder how busy people find time for involvement in projects like this. I did a little pecking around and found out that Luke Feck was a member of the Board of Directors of the Thurber House and while in Cincinnati where he was editor of the Cincinnati Enquirer, he was a member of the Literary Club. Knowing his background, I was able to understand Feck's passion for this project.

For more than 60 years, the house was a home to other families and was occasionally used for commercial purposes, including as a rooming house and beauty shop. It had not been kept up. The Thurber House Museum renovation took place in 1984 and I loved being a part of this wonderful project.

The Thurber House where I punched a hole in the ceiling to fit in a sofa in the writer's apartment in the attic of the museum.

Shortly after the Thurber House project, Gordy called me into his office and put me to work on a condo in West Palm Beach Florida for Mel and Irv, prominent builders in town. The conversation went like this: "Bea, you are being brought in for this project because they bought the condo for the enjoyment of both families, and they decided to keep the wives uninvolved in the decorating of the condo." Gordy went on to say one of the wives was probably capable of doing the whole condo herself but they thought it best that neither of the two wives should have the pleasure. I was the "it" girl for this job.

I met up with them in my office to get my marching orders. A king size bed in the master bedroom and twin beds in the guest room and the rest was up to me. They arranged plane fare for me and my husband to fly down there for the preliminary look. Gordy must have told them my husband was an architect.

Steve and I spent four days in West Palm Beach at the Breakers Hotel where the condos were located, and we measured every nook and cranny of the spaces. We measured the walls that would be papered, measured the windows for window treatments and met several times with the gal who managed the condos as my point person in case I had other questions once I returned to Columbus. She would be responsible for letting workers in and out for painting, and any other thing I might need done once I flew back to Ohio.

I went to work on the floor plans for the condo and when I completed everything, I presented it to Gordy before I called Mel and Irv to my office for their presentation. Everybody was on board and my clients approved of my designs. I went to work writing up the sales slips for the White's portion of the job. After Gordy worked on special pricing, I got the go ahead on completing this whole job.

Gordy and I made it clear to them that when every piece of furniture and accessories were in our warehouse, White's would then load our truck and we would drive the merchandise to Florida. I remember calling Mel on several occasions for more money as I went over budget on a few items. He always approved with a question: "When will it be done?"

Mel called me with an interesting add on task to the job. I was to go to Polsky's restaurant supply and furnish the kitchen. No budget, just do it and whatever I picked out would be packed and shipped to White's to go to the condo when we made the delivery.

It was kind of fun. I picked out dishes, silverware, cooking utensils, pots and pans and anything else they might need to function in the kitchen. Mel did tell me that he was related to the owners of Polsky's so they would be very accommodating. His wife called me one day and put me in touch with The Linen Store in Bexley for all the bedding and pillows and everything else I might need to finish off the bedrooms and bathrooms. She requested cotton sheets only and told me not to worry about expenses because she had an account with them. I found that to be a lot more fun than equipping the kitchen. They wanted to walk into the condo turnkey. In other words, nothing would be left to be done when they got there.

I made all necessary arrangements for the long-distance delivery. White's driver, along with my 18-year-old son Bill, drove the merchandise down to Florida and I was there to meet them for the set up. I pointed as things came off the truck and the condo began taking shape. Everything went along smoothly until we got to the mirrored three-piece wall unit. Each piece of the wall unit was set in place about 18 inches from the wall according to my drawing and I did not realize that the three heavy pieces needed to be bolted together. Bill and the delivery guy bolted the three pieces of heavy furniture together and we plugged in the lighted shelf units, and we realized that we were not able to push them in place against the wall. They were too heavy. What were we going to do?

I thought there might be a way. The three of us laid on our backs and pushed with our feet and very slowly we were able to snuggle the three pieces that were bolted together to the wall. Whew. Things were now in place. The truck headed back to Columbus, and I proceeded to finish the details. I set up the kitchen, made the beds, and took the wrappings off the lamp shades and did all the other things that needed done. There was only one thing left to do. It was requested that I use live plants in the condo and more live greenery to be placed on the patio.

I called on the building manager for advice and she put me in touch with a nursery. Once the plants were in place I was done. I called Mel and said the job was complete. I kicked back at the hotel and packed for my trip home.

A few weeks later I received a call from Mel and he very clearly said in three words, "We love it." His wife also called me and personally praised me and thanked me. It doesn't get any better than that for me.

By now, you are probably wondering how I managed to feed two teenagers, while working long retail hours. It was a bit clever of me; I suggested they find jobs in the food industry. Bill got a job as a busboy at an upscale restaurant. He would come home telling me that a lot of women ordered filet mignon and often they would only eat a few bites of it. When he cleared the table, he would put the steak in the microwave to nuke the germs and eat it. After bussing tables for a while he got a job on the grill at Bob Evans. I went to the counter often and was amazed how he would crack eggs with one hand and cook a dozen at one time while juggling the hash browns and sausage on the same grill. He was innovative in the kitchen and this skill has never left him.

Glen's work history was a bit different. He wanted to be an usher at the theater like a few of his school friends. I learned he ate a lot of nachos and cheese. He and Darren stepped up in the work world when they both got jobs in the kitchen at the Groveport Country Club. They used to come home and brag about the delicious banquet food they ate while working in the kitchen.

I was a lucky mom raising two sons and welcoming Darren into our family shortly after marrying Steve. All three boys were charged with doing their own laundry and pretty much feeding themselves. The only arguments about food was when one of them would get into the other's leftover pizza that was being saved in the refrigerator. Steve was talented. He could build shelves, remodel our kitchen, and he restored a 1940 pickup truck and rebuilt the Corvette engine in it. But, he did NOT know how to boil water. His idea of a home cooked meal was to eat peanuts while standing over the sink. BTW, peanuts are a good protein source. No one ever went hungry while I was a working mom and Steve agreed to always clean the kitchen whenever I cooked.

CHAPTER 17

MY PARK TOWERS ADVENTURE

Most mornings I sat down at the counter at Bob Evans with the newspaper and a cup of coffee before I headed to work. I called this part of my day "Bea Time." I recently married a wonderful man named Steve, the boys are in school, and I had just completed two fraternity houses on campus. Life is good.

I briefly glanced through the paper before going to the crossword puzzle and something caught my attention.

I read an article about a high-rise apartment building in Bexley that was going through a complete remodel upgrade. The article went on to say that a developer from Chicago bought the building.

They were putting the lobby and two model apartments into a competition open to the design community in Columbus. The lobby was included in the project to make sure the public would have a good impression of the building as they entered.

The article went on to explain they would have a team of experts from Chicago to judge the entries to determine who in Columbus would win the bid to design and decorate these three spaces.

This article kept my attention as I proceeded to do my crossword puzzle.

When I arrived at work that day and re-read the article about Park Towers, I casually waltzed into Gordy's office with the article and gave it to him. I asked him to read it and asked him to get back to me regarding the article. I wanted his input. He got back to me later in the day and said he did not care if I wanted to "go for it". He went on to say, "Remember Bea, you can't dance every dance." I took that as a go. And go I went. I filled out the application that was necessary and had Gordy sign the contract that stated that if Bea Gardner from White's Fine Furniture were to be selected for the job, White's was responsible. Gordy signed the paperwork and he and I never talked about Park Towers after that until a much later date.

I thought about the job for a few days and a lot was running through my mind on how and when and where to begin. I made an appointment with the principals and set up a time to look at the three spaces to be furnished. They walked me through the models in question. A two bedroom and a one-bedroom apartment were to be fully furnished. I was told that the parquet floors would be gone and they wanted the models to

My Park Towers Adventure

be carpeted. Well, that's easy enough I thought. I asked them if I could set up a time to measure the spaces.

It was then they told me this job must be kept very quiet to the existing residents because…. Then I got the real scoop. This firm from Chicago bought the building and they were planning to convert these apartments into condominiums. The reason for the secrecy was because a lot of the tenants were from the upscale community of Bexley and were elderly. The families set up their elderly parents in Park Towers and would not want to be forced to purchase their apartments, which was about to happen once the conversion took place.

That was what the developers were going to do and they were not going to upset their applecart until it was time to do so. In other words, kick out the old folks if they chose not to buy their units once the conversion went into effect. The most well-known tenant was Mrs. Amy Lazarus from the Lazarus Department Store. She lived on the top floor and was the "Queen" of the Towers, so to speak.

I went on with my usual sales floor schedule at White's and decided to proceed with this competition on my days off. I set up a time to measure and get into the mindset of designing these spaces. I did not want anyone at White's to question me about where I was and what I was doing at this time. Part of this was due to the developer's secrecy and partly because I also knew about my own competitive nature. I wanted to give myself time to allow my creative juices to flow before I started to layout the job and I wanted my own secrecy to stay intact because ultimately, I knew I was competing with the entire design community in Columbus and did not want anyone to know this. In other words, I did not want to brag about a big deal unless the big deal was mine to brag about. Thus, the competition began.

And, as you might remember, I started my career because of a design competition and I am and always have been a very competitive person. I was still just a "hybrid designer" in a retail furniture store.

The one-bedroom apartment came easily for me. I did my design as if I were designing for a young single bachelor who wanted to live in a high rise in a near downtown location. I geared the design and furnishings of the two-bedroom apartment for an elderly woman.

I spent more time in these three spaces than Gordy would have liked me to but that's just the way I am. I love doing a project when there is no client. Just pure design on my part. By the time I finished I had the two apartments and the lobby complete for the presentation. Each piece of product was priced out and written up for Gordy's approval. I had the carpet prices factored in since White's did not carry carpet. Same for the window treatments and wall coverings. I figured I would need to add at least 15% for accessories and I submitted the completed project to the Chicago firm. I submitted the project in its entirety with my bottom line included.

I recall during my presentation being asked why I gave an elderly woman a two-bedroom apartment. I told them two reasons went through my mind during the design process. I thought about an elderly woman wanting a second bedroom for her family who might be living out of town or her grandchildren to have a place to stay when they visited and/or a second bedroom could be used for in-home health care. I think I impressed them with my answer. They asked a few more questions. They liked the idea of mirroring the entire wall in the dining room of the bachelor pad to make the small space look larger and that was the end of my presentation. Their parting words were, "We will contact you if you are selected." That was it.

Many weeks went by and I contacted them to find out if they had made their selection and they responded that they were still not complete with their interviews. It was not too long after that phone call when I received a letter telling me that they were still in the process of selecting the person who would get the job, but they wanted me to know I was in the final few who were being considered. I showed Gordy the letter and he was elated and anxious for the final selection to be announced. At that time, my estimate for the job was in the $100,000 range for product and accessories. I waited for the call and in the meantime, Steve and I were soon to leave for a two-week cruise. I never heard from them and my husband and I left for the cruise with Gordy being the one they were to notify if I were to win the bid/contest.

Well, you guessed it. I won the competition and from what I heard, Gordy was about to explode with excitement and he was really antsy about not being able to contact me as I was sailing around the British Virgin Islands, with no communication to the real world.

When I returned, I got a call from Gordy before I even went to work the next day and he told me about the letter of acceptance I received from the Chicago firm. It was a little bit of a letdown because they split the job in two. The two models that I presented were awarded to me and the lobby was given to another designer. The total sales order for the two apartments was $67,000 in White's merchandise, the largest single sale the company ever had.

The two apartments were a testament to Bea Gardner, Interior Designer and a showcase for White's furniture in the heart of Bexley. My being the competitive person that I was, I was slightly disappointed that I did not get the lobby as well.

I still had my hands full because now I had to do the job. To pull this off to completion, Gordy and I went to work with a plan. Nothing would come off the sales floor. All the furniture would be special ordered and once I had all the sales slips and special orders completed the real design work began. I still needed to do the flooring, window treatments and accessories and get my quote for the mirrored wall.

Gordy decided I would be better off to shop for a lot of these things at the Merchandise Mart in Chicago. He booked me a flight to Chicago and gave me the company charge. Off I went.

For those of you who do not know the lay of the land I shall explain. The Merchandise Mart in Chicago is 25 floors

My Park Towers Adventure

tall consisting of showrooms with everything from furniture to carpets, lighting, fabrics, wallcoverings and wonderful accessories.

Prices are wholesale to the trades but that is a joke. Things were generally marked up by at least 40% to really give a 20% discount. But that's another discussion for another day.

My flight to Chicago departed at 8:00 am and with the time change I landed at Midway Airport in Chicago at 8:00 am. No luggage necessary. Just my briefcase with the room layouts as my guide.

The Mart opened at 9:00. What was I going to do for an hour? I did something that probably no other person in my position would do. I took the commuter bus to Downtown Chicago with a stop in front of the Merchandise Mart. The bus stopped every few blocks to pick up passengers and by the time we got about ¾ of the way to Downtown the bus was full. Mostly women I might add. A lot of them were carrying brown bag lunches, umbrellas, newspapers and books to read while riding the bus to work. One passenger was knitting. I had a great time people watching and even had an opportunity to talk to a few women on my bus trip to the Mart.

Once I got to the Mart, I checked myself in with all necessary credentials and off I went with the map of each floor in hand. I promised myself not to buy the first thing I saw and I carefully marked up the showroom and floor number of the places I would want to revisit. Off I went. I called this my Park Towers Adventure. It was fun and exhausting and very invigorating. I had a ball. Somehow, I found time to get a bite to eat before flying back to Columbus that day.

During the preliminary design process, I had the mirrored wall in the "bachelor pad" apartment installed and the carpets were laid in both units. Window treatments were in the workroom and the paperhanger had just finished hanging the wallpaper in the kitchen of the two-bedroom model.

Two horrific things happened almost simultaneously. The mirrored wall fell down. Honestly, it literally slipped off the wall and glass shattered all over the parquet floor.

In the two-bedroom model the old parquet flooring under the carpet was buckling. I called the principles and we visited these two issues. JR, the well-known mirror guy in town, was on the scene with us. It was determined that there was moisture between the walls from the adjoining apartment and JR figured out a solution. He would wallpaper the wall with a heavy wallpaper liner and then re-install the mirrors. JR agreed to re-do if the Chicago bigwigs agreed to pay for the materials. He would donate the labor this time around. That was settled.

Now, getting back to the carpet that was buckling because of the parquet tiles underneath causing this to happen. Again, the Chicago bigwig solved that problem. We would tear up the carpet and scrape up the parquet tiles in both the one bedroom and the two-bedroom apartments. The carpet was then re-laid. Whew, I dodged the bullet on both issues and was able to complete the two apartments as planned.

My Park Towers Adventure

I remembered asking them what to do with the flooring after removal and they said, "In the trash bin."

Did I mention Steve and I were married for about a year when I began this project? One thing Steve and I loved to do was go trashing, or what we called "dumpster diving." If you guessed right, you would know we loaded his pick-up truck with the parquet squares. We stacked them in piles in the garage, and one by one we scraped off the old glue and did his kitchen floor in this beautiful teak parquet.

We cleaned and polished and waxed that floor when completed and Glen had the perfect place to practice his "break dancing" gyrations.

I did a walk through and put the finishing touches on both models right before the grand opening event. I fluffed pillows, straightened pictures and made sure all lamp cords were hidden (a Gordy pet peeve). I put the signage in place in both models which read….This model apartment is tastefully furnished by White's Fine Furniture, Bea Gardner – Interior Designer, under my picture.

The only thing left to do was bask in our glory at the opening party that was held for the press and the residents with their dog and pony show explaining the condos convert and the price structure of the units.

I invited Gordy and his lovely wife Felice to the grand opening as well as my handsome husband Steve. The "Queen" of the Towers, Amy Lazarus, took to all of this like a champ. The most notable person I met while doing this job was Bob

Greene, an American journalist and author and well-known columnist with the Chicago Tribune, who was a relative of the "Queen." He came to the opening with his lovely parents who I chatted with on many occasions during my time on the job.

My Park Towers job was the single highest sale of merchandise ever recorded at White's. I remember spending days writing up the sales slips and special orders. At that time, I was happy to admit that I was glad not to have been awarded the lobby in addition to the two model apartments. I was proud but anxious to put this job to bed.

Park Towers in Bexley. I made the largest sale White's ever had when I ordered the furniture that I placed in the two model apartments I completed for the apartment to condo conversion.

My Park Towers Adventure

Yes, it is a fact that I got my start in this business with the winning room design at the Polsky's Department Store in Akron, Ohio and it is a fact that my largest sale came from my winning the design competition to decorate and furnish the two model apartments at Park Towers in Bexley, Ohio.

It is coincidental that my first job in my design/sales career was with the Lazarus Department Store in Akron, Ohio and the fact that in the penthouse apartment at the Park Towers apartments lived Amy Lazarus, mother of the owners of the Lazarus Department Stores.

By the way, did I mention she was a very attractive and keen elderly lady, probably in her 80's, and she never missed an opportunity to flirt with my handsome husband?

Let this be a lesson to all who aspire to be an interior designer. The best designs in the world will not be implemented until you are able to sell your look to the client. I believe my sales ability to explain why I decorated these two models the way I did was the reason I won the design contest for Park Towers. And because I won the bid, I was able to present Gordy with the largest single sale in the history of White's.

CHAPTER 18

THE END OF AN ERA

It was October in the year 1984. Things we tense in the room. I am not talking about a George Orwell book report. This was the day the selections were made to determine which room would be awarded to the designers participating in the Decorators' Show House.

It was a very important day for the design community. Viewing the finished room in the Decorators' Show House could be compared to strutting down the catwalk during a fashion show in Paris. The runway models displayed the best of the best of all the well-known clothing designers and a room being viewed in the Decorators' Show House did the same for interior designers.

The tenseness in the room was because of the big glass fish bowl that was sitting on a little table in the front of the room. The best of the best Interior Designers in the city of Columbus

The End of an Era

waited in anticipation for the drawing to begin. I did not know most of them. I was in my own little bubble in the world of designers. I never quite fit into their world. I always knew they were a snobby, "clickish" bunch, and this was the first time I was in the same room with most of them.

They sat in the chairs almost in an interior design pecking order. The ones who thought they were the best in town sat in the front row while I gravitated to the back of the room and watched this show of egos begin.

With this "clicky" group of high fluting designers I knew I did not fit. I worked for a furniture store and their attitudes clearly let it be known that I was not considered to be qualified to do any room in the Decorators' Show House.

In the past, this snobby group of designers would talk amongst themselves and decide who would do what room. I'll take the bedroom one would say and another would say I would like to do the living room. I think I'd like to do the study and someone else might pick the foyer. That's the way it was done in the past.

My mind started to wander a bit while little groups started to form in the room. I could see with my own eyes why Gordy did not bother to have White's participate in years past. White's and I did not exactly fit in with this crowd. I remember Gordy putting the invitation to participate in the Decorators' Show House in my box. I looked it over. After a few days of thinking about the letter asking White's if they wanted to participate, I approached Gordy about it. I told Gordy I'd like to do this.

"What do you think?" I asked. "We get this invitation to participate every year and I have not found it to be our thing," he replied.

I was saddened by his remark and naive, however I took the time to re-read the letter with the invitation to participate. A few days later I told Gordy I would like to throw my hat in the ring. He said, "Bea, you can't dance every dance." He told me that a lot. I said I know but what is there to lose? Gordy reluctantly agreed to let me follow through with the invitation to participate. He signed my application. And here I am, playing a part in this spectacle.

I jerked myself back to the moment when the committee chair of the Museum of Art began by getting our attention. She welcomed us. She then began to explain the numbered rooms on the blueprint of the house. The floor plan was prominently placed on an easel next to the fishbowl filled with all the applicants' names in it for everyone to see.

She began talking about several pertinent timelines during the decorating process and she really had the attention of the room when she began to explain the lottery system which was to be the "new" rules of selection.

The committee of women from the Columbus Museum of Art decided to make selections fair for everyone during the selection process, therefore, she explained, they decided to select by using a lottery system. She pointed to the fishbowl and told us the first name drawn from the bowl had first choice of what room they wanted to decorate and so on until all the

The End of an Era

available rooms were accounted for. She then pointed to the large blueprint on the easel next to the fishbowl and explained the numbering of the rooms would be noted as you selected a room if your name were to be drawn.

With much anticipation and trepidation, the drawing began. The first name drawn was a female designer who had a very good reputation in town. She chose the master bedroom suite.

The next name drawn from the bowl, drum roll please, was Bea Gardner, White's Fine Furniture. I was overcome with fear and excitement as I nervously walked to the front of the room. I hesitated for a moment as I looked over the blueprint. It didn't take me long to say..."I'll take the living room". You could feel the moans and murmurs from the crowd when my name was called. *Who is Bea Gardner?* the crowd must have been thinking. Most in this room had never heard of me.

One of the most revered interior designers who had his studio in a big old mansion on East Broad Street sat through the whole selection process until his name was finally called with only a bathroom left to do. He got up and it looked like he was walking to the front of the room to put his name on the blueprint when he turned towards the exit and said, "I'm out!" And out he went along with a few of his cronies who did not get their names drawn. They certainly did not like the lottery selection system.

This system of fairness put me on cloud nine when I left. I couldn't wait to get back to White's and spread the news to Gordy. I relayed the whole selection scene to him. I told Gordy I received a cold shoulder from the old guard of designers but that didn't scare me about decorating the room. And, to make matters even more interesting, the Show House was situated between Gordy's house and his close friend Les Wexner, about two or three houses in each direction and catty corner from the Governor's mansion in Bexley.

Very soon after the room selections were made, we received a letter from the Columbus Museum of Art inviting us designers to borrow any paintings we might want to incorporate in our settings from their Beaux Arts Gallery. It didn't take me long to realize that a painting from the museum would enhance my living room a lot better than any of the over-couch paintings I might find at White's.

I made it a point to visit the Beaux Arts Gallery before anyone else might consider doing so. I selected two large canvases from the Museum to incorporate into my room setting. One painting was a 50X60 oil on canvas valued at $8,500 and the other was a 38X46 oil on canvas valued at $6,000. Both were beautifully framed. I very quickly proceeded to visualize a color scheme based on these two paintings while filling out the paperwork for the museum to hang these in my room at set up time. I now had my color scheme before I began drawing the furniture layout. It was a good start.

At this early stage I never had any doubts about my ability to put this large awkward room together. There was very little unimpaired wall space in the room so I immediately knew I would have to float most of the furniture. A fireplace, built in shelving in two different areas of the room, windows awkwardly

The End of an Era

situated, a large opening into the room and a doorway out to the sunroom were some of the obstacles.

There was one wall that was badly damaged with about a two-foot hole in it. I took Gordy to look at it and to inform him that we would need to plaster the hole before I could set the painters to work. His mind was working and he finally said to me, "Why don't you use a folding screen on that wall?" He was a genius. I did indeed place a four panel, beautifully painted, silk screen on that wall and it laid out perfectly in the room. Problem solved.

Folding screen that I covered up the hole in the wall in the living room at the Decorators' Show House.

As my floor plan started to materialize, I knew I was on my way to making my name well known in the Columbus design community.

We were given two days to measure our rooms. As has always been my strong point, I usually can somewhat visualize what I will do before I even scale a room.

Me posing in my finished room in Decorators' Show House 1985. The White's sign is prominently placed on shelf over my shoulder

Shortly after our scheduled measurement days, the committee from the museum held a formal attire cocktail party for all the designers and their significant others. I was escorted by

The End of an Era

my handsome husband Steve. He looked dashing in his stylish double-breasted tuxedo and, if I do say so myself, I looked marvelous in my cocktail attire. I thought it was a cool tradition to have a formal event in the un-decorated house.

There was another cocktail party, a pre-opening gathering, to show off the finished rooms before opening day. That was the only time I was able to view the finished rooms of all the other designers. It was not a formal event. During that cocktail party we were given tickets to purchase so that we could give them away to friends and family or sell them. They were sold to us for $5.00 each and if they were to be purchased at the door by the public the tickets cost $6.00 each. Remember this was the year 1985.

The last major event sponsored by the museum committee was what they called Designer's Market. When our rooms were completed, we designers had to turn in a detailed inventory of every item in the room. Itemized on page one was a list of the major pieces of furniture. Page two contained a list of miscellaneous items such as carpet and window treatments and the art and sculpture that was used in the design. Page three consisted of miscellaneous accessories.

These lists became the instrument for the committee to sell any individual item from the lists to the public when the show ended. The Market Days were held on May 14th and 15th. On list number three, every item was discounted 30% to the public. As I recall, a lot of expensive silk plants were sold. People from the public flocked to the sale and a lot of things got sold from my room. The remaining room furniture and accessories were picked up by the White's truck the following day and were merged into White's inventory.

Designers' Show Houses are held all over the country as fundraisers. The money raised from ticket sales to the public and sales from the Designer's Market were donated to the Columbus Museum of Art.

From the beginning to the end of this project was about nine months. From the time I told Gordy I wanted to participate to the tear down day, it was like birthing my beautiful baby, the living room in the Decorators' Show House.

I have accomplished everything I ever imagined possible as an Interior Designer. I was able to put a roof over my kids' heads while selling furniture on the sales floor at White's and decorated rooms for hundreds of White's customers. I designed and furnished two Ohio State fraternity house lounges. I decorated six community room lounges at a nursing home and completed models in several Parade of Homes. I won the bid to decorate two models at the Park Towers when a firm from Chicago bought the building to convert the units from apartments to condominiums.

I reached a huge milestone in my career when I decorated the living room in the show house. I have come from winning a design contest in Akron, Ohio with no education in the business, to be at the top of my field when my work was showcased to thousands of visitors during the 1985 Decorators' Show House.

The End of an Era

I posted my Decorators' Show House sign with my picture on it, in my office. The sign read… Living room designed by Bea Gardner, White's Fine Furniture.

My parenting days were almost over. Bill was off to college and I got married. Steve taught me to play golf, and it didn't take long before I was hooked on the game. We joined Little Turtle Country Club while Glen and Darren were thriving in high school. They were not interested in learning the game of golf.

I left White's employ shortly after the teardown of the Decorators' Show House and went to work for Lombard's. I decided to slow down a bit with the hustle of selling and wanted to concentrate on just being a designer. Lombard's was a full-service store with a complete design studio. Wallcoverings, carpets, and window treatments were all under one roof and it sure made a design job in progress a whole lot easier than doing one at White's. And the commission structure was a lot better than White's. I spent two years at Lombard's until Steve and I moved permanently to Florida.

I will be forever grateful to Gordy for having faith in me and sticking it out with me during my first 10 years in Columbus and my employment at White's. Gordy will forever hold a warm spot in my heart.

AFTERWORD

Glen, Darren, and Bill circa 1984

Bill graduated from college, Glen was serving in the Navy and Darren was in his first year of college. Steve and I had moved to Florida. We wanted to establish ourselves in Florida before we were too old to enjoy it. That was the end of my

Afterword

formal interior design career. I knew I would not be able to bring my reputation as a top-notch designer with me, so I found other things to keep me busy.

I opened a secondhand furniture and accessory store and named it Encore Furniture. It was much like a consignment shop but I owned all my merchandise outright. Steve and I found merchandise at estate sales, garage sales and went to flea markets within a 100-mile radiance. We even found some cool things on the curb in an affluent neighborhood the night before their trash pickup.

Faux finishes and custom painted furniture became all the rage and I put my artistic skills to work in that arena. I remember buying two nightstands at a garage sale for $10.00 a pair and put my creative mind to work. I painted them and sold the pair for $300.00. I was on my way. The back room of my shop became my artist's studio. When a piece was completed, I featured it on the sidewalk to lure customers in. I have three scrapbooks full of pictures of my painted furniture.

An eclectic array of interesting pieces of furniture from antique to mid-century modern could be found in my shop. Deco furniture flew out as quickly as I could find some.

My shop was situated in the middle of Downtown Vero Beach and I served on the board of the Downtown Vero Beach Association (DVBA). I was VP of fundraising and I gathered a committee of 22 and we created an event called Downtown Friday. The event is now 30 years old and still going strong in Downtown Vero Beach.

Bought these two night stands at a garage sale for $5.00 each. Sold the pair for $300.00 after painting them.

Painted headboard that I bought at Salvation Army Store and painted the lamp shades to go with it. I don't remember what I sold it for.

After Downtown Friday I became active in so many other things that I decided to close up my little store and I took a

Afterword

part-time job with Ethan Allen. Yes, I was again a Hybrid Designer, working in sales and design three days a week. It's in my blood. I stayed there for 18 months but it was never the same for me. Not a Gordy in sight is the best way I can describe it.

I dabbled in politics and I ran for office several times but never won. Close but no cigar, as they say. I continued to serve the city and the county in various roles and loved meeting the people. I spent 16 years on the Parks and Recreation Commission for the City of Vero Beach and was President of the Republican Club of Indian River County for four years. I wrote a blog called Bea-isms and had a radio spot once a week to rehash what I was writing on my blogs.

Suddenly tragedy hit home. Steve was diagnosed with Alzheimer's Disease and he had just had his first stroke to pile on to the sadness in my life. I knew it was time to head back to Ohio to be closer to family while caregiving for a disease that had a long goodbye. After 36 years of marriage, Steve passed. It was then that I turned to writing.

When I returned to Columbus, White's was no longer in business and soon after that, Gordy passed away. I never had a chance to say a proper goodbye. Throughout my career he was always my mentor, my inspiration and my friend and that is the reason I have dedicated this book to him. I will be forever grateful to Gordy for having faith in me and being my friend while in his employ.

Gordy's son Andy has put together "White's Alumni Reunions" about once a year and I look forward to them. At the first reunion I said hi to an unfamiliar face. "I worked at White's a long time ago and I feel pretty sure we did not work there at the same time," I said. She told me her name was Kari and she did not recognize me either and asked me my name. "I'm Bea Gardner," I said. She kind of stepped back a bit and looked me in the eye and said, "Oh, I've heard of you." I had been gone from White's for about 40 years when I went to this reunion.

That was the first of a few Alumni gatherings. It was really cool to meet up with a few old timers and some of the others who worked for White's over the years. It made me proud to know that my reputation was still talked about by a few of these people who attended and it certainly brought back memories.

Dan was a friend I had made when he and I worked together at White's and Lombard's. I was excited when I saw him at the reunion. He was still as soft spoken and handsome as ever. He was happy to see me and was excited to introduce me to his new husband. Wow, Dan got married. I was happy for him.

I moved around the room all evening meeting up with new faces and loved catching up with some of the old familiar faces in the room. I talked to Buddy, one of the floor salesmen I worked with. When I approached him, I thought to myself, I'll bet he sits on the porch chewing his gum in an old rocking chair and probably hunts deer in camo clothes. How wrong I was. Buddy left White's and became a very successful appliance

Afterword

salesman for Sears. And no, he did not deer hunt. He spent his retirement as a day trader in the stock market and has been very successful in this endeavor. I asked him what he does as a hobby, like Pickleball or something like that. He said he walks. He walks many miles every day and does his day trading and lives a quiet solo life. He really surprised me.

Another gal I worked with left her position with an offer to partner in a new startup company. One year later, the partnership had yet to materialize and she and her husband made a decision to go it alone in the office furnishings business. She is the success story that evolved after her 10 plus years at White's.

Larry Buttermore, my manager, left White's after 20 years and took a leap of faith and went into the insurance business with State Farm.

Larry got this plaque for his years of service.

Larry and Gordy's son Andy and I still get together between Alumni parties every few months for dinner. Mostly we exchange funny stories. At one time I asked Larry whatever happened to my friend Ron. We began to exchange some funny stories about Ron and Larry told me this one. Gordy called Ron into his office one day to put Ron in touch with one of his Country Club friends. He told Ron this friend and his family lived in one of the biggest homes in Bexley.

Ron made the house call. He rang the bell and was welcomed into a large foyer, and Ron went no further. He looked the lady of the house in the eye and said to her, "If you do not throw away those horrible plastic grapes in that bowl immediately, I will not go further into your house." OMG, I laughed so hard I could barely contain myself. That was Ron. Nothing that came out of his mouth would ever surprise me.

Winning the design contest in Akron and winning the bid to design the two apartments at Park Towers and winning the lottery in the selection of rooms at the 1985 Decorators' Show House certainly played a big part in my climb to fame as an Interior Designer. You might ask yourself, was my career based on luck or was I gifted with talent as an Interior Designer, or was it because I made the sacrifices and put in the hard work to make it happen? I believe it was all of the above.

My sons, and Steve's son who I always called "my other son," are grown and live in three different countries. I met a widower named Dave on the Pickleball court three years after Steve passed and we soon became a thing. He passed away four

Afterword

years later and I am left with fond memories of our short time together. Dave and I wrote a two act play called Widows at the Club. You can read about my book "Bring It On…We're In Our 70's" and the play Dave and I wrote on my website, www.beagardner.com.

I am halfway past my 84th birthday as I write my memoir, which centers on my design career. I never for one moment regretted my choice of the career path I took nor the years it took to reach the top.

My typical designeresque look. I'm so proud
I finally learned to use a scale ruler.

ACKNOWLEDGEMENTS

    I want to thank my son Glen Gardner and especially my granddaughter Kelsey Kerstetter Yahner, for her role as acting editor. Kelsey's masterful use of the English language and her keen eye for proper punctuation was invaluable to me as I wrote. Without her keeping me on track and organized I may never have completed The Hybrid Designer. Thank you Kelsey from the bottom of my heart.

    Hats off to Andy Schiffman, Gordon Schiffman's son and Larry Buttermore, my manager at White's, for their continuing contributions and support from the very beginning of my journey and for believing in my story and championing it tirelessly.

    I would like to acknowledge everyone who contributed to this project with special thanks to Helen MacMurray, Joy Rinehart, Barbara Sanderow, Ruth Embly, Pam Rako, Maxine

Acknowledgements

Weinberg and David Cohen. Your support has been invaluable, and I am truly grateful. Their eyes and ears on this book in progress was clearly a help to me during the writing process.

Writing a book, specifically centered around my sales and design career, has been harder than I thought and more rewarding than I could have ever imagined. None of my career would have been possible without Gordon Schiffman always being there when I needed him and I thank his son Andy for allowing me to use Gordy's real name while writing The Hybrid Designer.

Gordy stood by me during my struggles while parenting my two sons and kept a keen eye on my ability to sell and design. It took many years to accomplish my "wanna-be" Interior Designer dream to my prominent design office with the title of Bea Gardner, Corporate Designer, White's Fine Furnishings. For all of that, I will always be grateful to Gordon Schiffman.

ABOUT THE AUTHOR

In **The Hybrid Designer** Bea Gardner's memoir specifically relates to her career in furniture sales and interior design. "I began writing late in life and never thought of myself as a writer. She says, "I am, and always will be an Interior Designer".

Bea and her sons Bill and Glen water skied in competition while she pursued her career. She played pickleball for the past 8 years, long before it ever became the rage and she finally, at the age of 84 decided to give it a break to devote her time to write about her career.

About the Author

In **The Hybrid Designer** she specifically relates to her career in furniture sales and Interior Design and the struggles she faced as a single mom while building her career.

Bea surprised herself, at her late age, because the short-term memory is a little slow but, as she reached back 50 years to write **The Hybrid Designer** the stories became very clear. Her long-term memory was still intact. She challenges herself every Tuesday night with her weekly Texas Hold'em poker game.

In addition to **The Hybrid Designer** Bea Gardner is the author of "Bring It On…We're In Our 70's" and co-authored a two act play with her partner David Russell titled "Widows At the Club"

Bea was born in Canton, OH and spent most of her childhood in Cleveland. She lived in Vero Beach, FL for 25 years and now resides in New Albany, OH.

www.beagardner.com

www.ingramcontent.com/pod-product-compliance
Lightning Source LLC
Chambersburg PA
CBHW051102160426
43193CB00010B/1284